LIVERPOOL

Bill Day

Illustrated by Craig Warwick

Purnell

A PURNELL BOOK
Text © Bill Day 1988
Illustrations © Macdonald & Co (Publishers) Ltd 1988
First published in Great Britain in 1988
by Macdonald & Co (Publishers) Ltd
London & Sydney
A member of Maxwell Pergamon Publishing Corporation plc
All rights reserved

Macdonald & Co (Publishers) Ltd
Greater London House
Hampstead Road
London NW1 7QX

British Library Cataloguing in Publication Data

Day, Bill
 Liverpool.
 1. England. Association football. Clubs:
 Liverpool Football Club, (Association
 football), 1970–77 – Personal observations
 I. Title II. Series
 796.334′63′0942753

 ISBN 0-361-08490-0
 ISBN 0-361-08291-9 Pbk

Cover photograph: Colorsport

Typeset, printed and bound in Great Britain by
Hazell Watson & Viney Limited
Member of BPCC plc
Aylesbury, Bucks, England

Contents

Useful Addresses		4
Liverpool Honours		4
1987–88 League Record		5
Introduction		7
1	Early Days	9
2	Liddell on the Charge	20
3	Enter Emperor Shankly	27
4	You'll Never Walk Alone	36
5	Paisley's Pirates Run Riot	51
6	Kenny's Kings	69
7	Ten of the Best:	
	Billy Liddell	80
	Roger Hunt	81
	Ian St John	84
	Ray Clemence	85
	Kevin Keegan	87
	Graeme Souness	88
	Kenny Dalglish	89
	Ian Rush	91
	John Barnes	92
	Peter Beardsley	93
Index		95

Useful Addresses

Liverpool Football Club: Anfield Road, Liverpool L4 0TH

Supporters' Club Information: Administrator: Mr R. Gill, Liverpool Supporters' Club, Lower Breck Road, Anfield, Liverpool 6

There are many regional branches of the supporters' club. Write to the above person for details of the one nearest to you.

Liverpool Honours

League Division 1 Champions: 1901, 1906, 1922, 23, 47, 64, 66, 73, 76, 77, 79, 80, 82, 83, 84, 86, 88. (Liverpool have a record number of 17 League Championship wins)
FA Cup Winners: 1965, 74, 86
League Cup/Milk Cup Winners: 1981, 82, 83, 84
League Super Cup Winners: 1986
European Cup Winners: 1977, 78, 81, 84
UEFA Cup Winners: 1973, 76
Super Cup Winners: 1977

LIVERPOOL 1987–88 LEAGUE RECORD

Match	Date	Venue	Opponents	Result		Goalscorers
1	Aug 15	A	Arsenal	W	2-1	Aldridge, Nicol
2	29	A	Coventry C	W	4-1	Nicol 2, Aldridge (pen), Beardsley
3	Sept 5	A	West Ham U	D	1-1	Aldridge (pen)
4	12	H	Oxford U	W	2-0	Aldridge, Barnes
5	15	H	Charlton Ath	W	3-2	Aldridge (pen), Hansen, McMahon
6	20	A	Newcastle U	W	4-1	Nicol 3, Aldridge
7	29	H	Derby Co	W	4-0	Aldridge (2 pens), Beardsley
8	Oct 3	H	Portsmouth	W	4-0	Beardsley, McMahon, Aldridge, Whelan (pen)
9	17	H	QPR	W	4-0	Johnston, Aldridge (pen), Barnes 2
10	24	A	Luton T	W	1-0	Gillespie
11	Nov 1	H	Everton	W	2-0	McMahon, Beardsley
12	4	A	Wimbledon	D	1-1	Houghton
13	15	A	Manchester U	D	1-1	Aldridge
14	21	H	Norwich C	D	0-0	
15	24	H	Watford	W	4-0	McMahon, Houghton, Aldridge, Barnes
16	28	A	Tottenham H	W	2-0	McMahon, Johnston
17	Dec 6	H	Chelsea	W	2-1	Aldridge (pen), McMahon
18	12	A	Southampton	D	2-2	Barnes 2
19	19	H	Sheffield W	W	1-0	Gillespie
20	26	A	Oxford U	W	3-0	Aldridge, Barnes, McMahon
21	28	H	Newcastle U	W	4-0	McMahon, Aldridge 2 (pen), Houghton
22	Jan 1	H	Coventry C	W	4-0	Beardsley 2, Aldridge, Houghton
23	16	H	Arsenal	W	2-0	Aldridge, Beardsley
24	23	A	Charlton Ath	W	2-0	Beardsley, Barnes
25	Feb 6	H	West Ham U	D	0-0	
26	13	A	Watford	W	4-1	Beardsley 2, Aldridge, Barnes
27	27	A	Portsmouth	W	2-0	Barnes 2
28	Mar 5	A	QPR	W	1-0	Barnes
29	16	A	Derby Co	D	1-1	Johnston

(Equalled Leeds United's record run of 29 League game wins)

30	20	A	Everton	L	0-1	
31	26	H	Wimbledon	W	2-1	Aldridge, Barnes
32	April 2	A	Nottingham F	L	1-2	Aldridge (pen)
33	4	H	Manchester U	D	3-3	Beardsley, Gillespie, McMahon
34	13	H	Nottingham F	W	5-0	Houghton, Aldridge 2, Gillespie, Beardsley
35	20	A	Norwich C	D	0-0	
36	23	H	Tottenham H	W	1-0	Beardsley

(Liverpool clinched the Championship with this game)

37	30	A	Chelsea	D	1-1	Barnes
38	May 2	H	Southampton	D	1-1	Aldridge
39	7	A	Sheffield W	W	5-1	Johnston 2, Barnes, Beardsley 2
40	9	H	Luton T	D	1-1	Aldridge

Final League position: 1st

Introduction

THIS is the story of Liverpool Football Club, the most successful First Division Team in Football League history. It explores the Reds' phenomenal rise from near bankruptcy to fame for near perfection, both on and off the pitch.

'Let's do it the Liverpool way' has become a source of advice and inspiration to a host of players and clubs who try to copy the blueprint for Liverpool's astonishing trophy-winning run, which continued in the 1987–88 season with their Championship win for a record 17th time.

The book chronicles the history of the club from the big Scot Alex Raisbeck, their first big name star, to immaculate captain and fellow countryman Alan Hansen; from Elisha Scott, the hugely gifted goalkeeper, to Bruce Grobbelaar, the most colourful; from Billy Liddell, the flying Scot, to England wing-wizard John Barnes; from prolific goal-ace Albert Stubbins to deadly Ian Rush, and latterly the impudent England striker Peter Beardsley.

It captures the atmosphere of bleak winter nights warmed by the floodlit excitement of historic matches in European competition, climaxed by Liverpool's great European Cup winning exploits. It charts the Reds' stranglehold on the League Championship at the turn of the century and their record-breaking First Division campaigns of the last 25 years.

It explores the legend of Bill Shankly, the greatest single influence on Anfield in the club's long and glittering history. It covers the Paisley Years of win, win, win, and dwells on the desperate last moments of Joe Fagan's reign when the club suffered the blackest night in its history in the Heysel Stadium, Brussels.

Above all, this is a story of unrivalled triumph earning the highest praise in the 1987–88 season when Kenny Dalglish's kings were hailed the 'Team of the Century'.

Chapter One

Early Days

THE choir of the Kop (as the massed supporters of Liverpool are named after the massive Spion Kop stand) has been in good voice for so long that it seems hard to believe that Liverpool Football Club could have emerged from very humble beginnings. But stormy controversy was as much a part of the club's life on Merseyside as any heady success. The late Tom Watson, a former secretary of the club, said once: 'Our life is full of trouble, we are always fighting for Championships, Cups or promotion, or else we are fighting to escape relegation.'

In mentioning the problems on the pitch, Mr Watson could have pointed an accusing finger in other directions. He could have spoken about the shame heaped on the club by a group of players who tried to 'fix' a game, or the panic that set in when a thief stole two magnificent trophies from the boardroom.

Quick success – and stolen silver

Liverpool, now recognised as one of the top six clubs in the world, has rarely failed to make headlines since their first game against Rotherham on 1 September, 1892. Liverpool won 7–1.

Liverpool had big ideas from the outset. They applied for Football League membership in their first season – a request that was refused, forcing the club to join the Lancashire Association.

Their first great manager was an Irishman named John McKenna, a rich bowler-hatted businessman who spoke sound football sense. His knowledge of players was unrivalled in the North, and he lost no time tapping a rich seam of talent after his arrival from his former home in Scotland.

As a result of McKenna's influence, the first team Liverpool ever fielded contained such names as McLean, McQueen, McBride and McVean. There was not a single Englishman in the line-up! To this day Liverpool teams have contained a healthy sprinkling of Scots and Irish talent.

Malcolm McVean, captain from the crack Scottish club Third Lanark, had the honour of scoring Liverpool's first ever goal, and Liverpool went on to crown an outstanding first season by landing a League and Cup Double in the Lancashire League. They won 17 of their 22 matches, scoring more than 60 goals and conceding fewer than 20.

Their Double celebrations were sadly interrupted when police were called to investigate the theft of the two silver cups they had paraded in the boardroom. The trophies were never recovered and Liverpool, still not a rich club, with poor home support, had to spend £150 to replace the silverware.

Spurred by his team's success, McKenna made a second application for the club to join the Football League after hearing that Accrington Stanley had quit the Second Division. This time the determined and ambitious McKenna succeeded and on 2 September 1893, just one year and one day after their first game against Rotherham, Liverpool beat Middlesbrough away 2–0 in their first League encounter, in the Second Division.

Who should have the honour of scoring Liverpool's first League goal? None other than the same inspirational captain, McVean, who had scored their first Lancashire League goal the previous season.

Home support
Liverpool had been attracting large audiences at away matches, but it was not until they launched their Football League campaign that the workforces of the city's factories and shipbuilding wharves began to support them. Five thousand watched the team beat Lincoln 4–0 in their first League game at Anfield. 27 matches later they were at the top of the Division and still unbeaten, winning 22 games and scoring 77 goals.

Gates of 20,000 saw Liverpool struggle to make an impact the following season in the First Division. They lost four and drew four of their first eight matches, but spirits were high when they faced Everton in the first Merseyside derby on 13 October, 1895. Liverpool took the game so seriously that they went to Hightown for a week's training. The Lord Mayor was among the 44,000 people packed into Goodison to see whether Liverpool's uncompromising toughies could upset the aristocrats from over the road. Everton won 3–0, but they were pegged to a 2–2 draw in the return at Anfield later in the season.

(It still irks Liverpool supporters to know that Everton, deadly Merseyside rivals, played at Anfield *before* the Reds. Everton, as the first major football club on Merseyside was named in 1879, had played at Anfield for eight years before they decided to leave the ground, after arguments with its owner, for a new pitch at nearby Goodison Park.)

Determined to win

Liverpool's first season ended in bitter disappointment and relegation, but typical of the grim determination that was to illustrate their League campaigns in future years, manager McKenna swore: 'We will return'. And sure enough, they topped the Second Division again in 1896 and were to remain a First Division force until 1904.

The 'new' Liverpool was built round a young striker named George Allan, from Leith Athletic in Scotland. He cracked four goals in a 10–1 victory over Rotherham in the 1895–96 season, a feat acknowledged by Scotland when he was chosen to play against England in 1897. Tragically, he died at the age of 24.

Harry Bradshaw became the first Liverpool player to be capped by England (v Ireland in 1897), and a few months later Liverpool's new signing from Preston North End, Frank Becton, joined him in the England team.

Rab Howell, who lived in a gypsy caravan, was one of Liverpool's more colourful players of this period; but their first major star was Alex Raisbeck, a spring-heeled centre-half whose 5ft 9ins frame could be seen towering above forwards in any game. He became one of the outstanding defenders at the turn of the century.

Manager McKenna had now been joined by Sunderland secretary Tom Watson, and that partnership was to become as effective as the boardroom-dressing room link that Kenny Dalglish and Peter Robinson share today.

Liverpool were firm favourites to clinch their first Championship in 1898–99. They led the table with three games to go. All depended on their final game against title rivals Aston Villa. It was Liverpool's 16th game in 43 days: their players looked whacked – and they were whacked 5–0! And Sheffield United destroyed their Cup dream, so Liverpool ended the season smarting from what-might-have-been.

Liverpool were not to be denied success for long. They won their first Championship in 1900–1, a title they were to clinch 17 times in the next 88 years. But in typical see-saw fashion, by February they had hardly looked like champions. Their defence had leaked 31 goals and they had been beaten eight times. However, they embarked on a storming run of 12 unbeaten matches. And so Raisbeck was lifted shoulder high with the Championship trophy raised aloft!

The Club faced personal sadness and loss in 1902 when John Houlding, a former Mayor and the man who founded Liverpool, died. He had been associated with Liverpool for 20 years. Residents stood bare-headed in front of their terrace houses when his funeral cortège slid by quietly, with both Liverpool and Everton players acting as pall-bearers.

Liverpool in Paris!
A maximum £4 wage was introduced throughout the League, but Liverpool's huge gates enabled them to make bonus payments. Alex Raisbeck was their highest earner, a tribute to his skill and Liverpool's determination to beat off several bids for his services from other clubs.

In 1903-4 they were relegated again, and squabbles over money destroyed team spirit. But, undaunted, a new stand was built in the hope of a swift return to the First Division, and Liverpool managed to regain their status at the first attempt. They were to remain in the top flight for the next 50 years.

Joe Hewitt cracked 23 goals to steer Liverpool to their second Championship in 1905-06, and they might have performed the magic League and Cup Double had Everton not halted their progress in the semi-finals of the F.A. Cup, but the team's title triumph was rewarded with a club holiday in Paris. The famous Spion Kop (named after a battle in 1900 during the Boer War in South Africa, in which the King's Regiment from Liverpool fought) was built but Liverpool were not to win another trophy for 16 years.

Personalities on the pitch
The team was struggling, but supporters took consolation in cheering the performances of individual stars of that age.

Ned Doig became the first of a host of great goalkeepers to wear the Liverpool jersey. After

Doig, keeper Sam Hardy crowned more than 200 appearances for the club by becoming an England regular.

Raisbeck retired in 1910 with two Championship medals on his sideboard, but James Harrop, a £250 bargain from Rotherham, became a worthy replacement for the Great Man.

With storm clouds brewing over Europe, Liverpool signed a young Irishman who was to become a goalkeeping legend at Anfield for the next 20 years. Elisha Scott was as colourful in his era as Bruce Grobbelaar was to become in another decade. Capped 31 times by Ireland, he made more than 450 appearances for Liverpool. He wore three sweaters, two pairs of socks, and became so embroiled in his battles with legendary Everton striker Dixie Dean that Merseyside folklore decrees that when they met in the street on their day off, Dean nodded a friendly 'good morning' – and Scott hurled himself across the street at an imaginary ball!

A stickler for preparation, Scott arrived for matches two hours before his team-mates and warmed up by hurling a football around the dressing room.

Ephraim Longworth, a Liverpool stalwart between 1910 and 1927, captained England from full-back and had the honour to lead Liverpool onto the Crystal Palace pitch where they made their first F.A. Cup Final appearance in 1914.

Royal hopes
King George V, the first reigning monarch to watch a Cup Final, was in the 72,000 crowd that watched Liverpool play Burnley. Some sup-

porters climbed telegraph poles outside the ground for free viewing, while others risked their necks at the tops of trees. Special trains steamed into the capital, bringing 20,000 Liverpool fans to the Final; but their cheers were to dry in their throats just before the end when Burnley's Freeman thundered a volley into Liverpool's net.

Those who thought King George's red buttonhole a lucky omen were cruelly denied. Little were they to know that not for another 36 years would Liverpool appear in an F.A. Cup Final.

Scandal breaks
The 1914–15 season was one of the worst in Liverpool's history. With match programmes asking for recruits to enlist in Lord Kitchener's army, and with players anticipating the postponement of League action for them to fight in the impending war, some of the Liverpool and Manchester United stars hatched a plan to throw a match after laying odds on the result at the bookies. They chose the Good Friday game against Manchester United, the Liverpool team hardly raising a sweat as they crashed to a 2–0 defeat. The *Sporting Chronicle* broke the scandal with an invitation for information for which they would pay a reward. The Football League investigation was damning, proving that 'a considerable sum of money changed hands by betting on the match and some of the players profited thereby.'

Four players from each club were banned for life. Liverpool's guilty men were Jack Sheldon, a former Manchester United player and the ringleader; the unfortunately named Tom Fairfoul; Tommy Miller, a former Motherwell, Third Lanark and Hamilton Academicals star; and Bob Purcell, who was poached from Queens Park in an illegal deal that had cost Liverpool a fine of £250. Happily, the Football League lifted the ban when the four Liverpool players returned from First World War service.

Between the wars
Liverpool snapped back into Championship winning form by lifting the title in two successive seasons, 1921–22 and 1922–23.

Goal-poachers Dick Forshaw (17 goals) and Harold Chambers (19) helped Liverpool crack 63 goals in the first of those title wins. Elisha Scott masterminded an almost impregnable defence in the second of those Championship triumphs, only 32 goals hitting Liverpool's net – a League record. Scott let in only 63 goals in 81 games over two seasons, and his was the first name to go on the team-sheet in a line-up that rarely changed and read thus: Scott, Longworth, McKinlay, McNab, Wadsworth, Bromilow, Lacey, Forshaw, Shone, Chambers and Hopkins.

But Everton were to dominate Merseyside between the two Wars as Liverpool's great manager John McKenna gave way to Matt McQueen, a regular from the team of the late 19th century. McKenna's 40 year association with the club ended in March 1936 when, at the age of 81, he died. A former President of the Football League and Vice-President of the F.A., no man did more for the club.

New talent and problem players

Liverpool's strong connections with Scotland were relaxed as the club began to scout for overseas talent. Arthur Riley, a member of the South African touring team of 1925, became Elisha Scott's successor in 1935, after almost 10 years in Liverpool's reserves.

Gordon Hodgson, another South African, joined in 1926 with a reputation for scoring goals and runs! A true sportsman, he combined playing football for Liverpool with regular appearances in Lancashire's Championship cricket team. Liverpool were winning nothing, but the Kop were not slow to respond to Hodgson's goal-scoring talents, especially in the 1930–31 season when he set a club record of 36 goals.

One of the most remarkable figures of the late twenties and early thirties was the Rev. James Jackson, a tough tackling full-back who drove discipline into the dressing room by warning team-mates of the dangers of gambling and alcohol.

Two England full-backs, Ernie Blenkinsop, from Sheffield Wednesday, and Tom Cooper, from Derby, arrived for £6000, and Tom Bradshaw, Scotland's centre-half for the famous 'Wembley Wizards', moved to Anfield from Bury for £8000.

Tom Johnson, another ex-England forward, was transferred from Barrow in 1935, and a certain Matt Busby, who was to become famous as manager of Manchester United in later life, was transferred from Manchester City.

Busby was to do Liverpool proud but the others

proved to be 'over the hill' when signed up for Liverpool. Blenkinsop and Cooper, for instance, arrived with more than 40 England caps between them, a figure they were unable to increase in their Anfield days.

Liverpool's least wise signing was of the unfortunate Irish international from Rangers, Sammy English. He had been driven out of Ibrox and the Scottish League in a storm of barracking after his accidental collision with Celtic goalkeeper John Thomson.

Thomson suffered a fractured skull and subsequently died, with English bearing the brunt of the blame. Heckled whenever he played, he sought escape at Anfield, cracking 18 goals in his first season. But for every cheer, he suffered the indignity of terrace abuse and walked out after just one season.

Everton's domination of Merseyside battles and major trophies was to upset Liverpool right through the thirties to the outbreak of the Second World War. It was then that a shaft of sunlight crept through the gloom at Anfield in the shape of a fresh-faced 18-year-old signing a contract in the secretary's office. The date was July 1938. The player? None other than Billy Liddell, a dynamic winger who was about to help turn Liverpool from a mediocre First Division club into a formidable Championship-winning machine.

Chapter Two

Liddell on the Charge

LIVERPOOL made one of the most remarkable signings in football history when boxer Joe Louis, the former World Heavyweight Champion, joined the Reds in 1944. Britain was beginning to celebrate the prospect of victory in the Second World War when Louis, known as the 'Brown Bomber', helped raise club morale when he visited on a trans-Atlantic tour. Liverpool captured the spirit of that occasion and, just for fun, invited Louis to sign a contract!

Later, Liverpool's pre-season tour of North America in the summer of 1946 soon convinced manager George Kay that he had the makings of a winning First Division team.

The main focus of Kay's interest centred on Billy Liddell, who had made his début for Liverpool in a 7–1 defeat of Crewe back in January 1940. Shortly after that opener he had scored a hat-trick against Manchester City, despite the massive presence of Frank Swift, the greatest goalkeeper of his generation.

There was no doubting Liddell's ability, but like so many of his contemporaries, his progress

Billy Liddell – the first of a long line of great wingers at Anfield.

had been slowed by lack of football activity in wartime. However, he made a great return to the game at the start of the 1946–7 season when he capitalised on a slipshod Chelsea defence. He crowned a remarkable League début by scoring twice in a 7–4 victory.

Tossing a coin for the team
A 5–0 defeat by Manchester United caused rare panic behind the scenes at Anfield, persuading manager Kay he needed to strengthen his squad. He went for Newcastle United's prolific goal-scoring talent Albert Stubbins – at the same time as Everton put in a bid for him!

Both clubs were prepared to splash out on what was then a British record fee of £12,500 for the Magpies' centre-forward. But Stubbins kept both Merseyside clubs waiting because he couldn't make up his mind which club he preferred to join. He tossed a coin – and Liverpool won!

Stubbins formed a lethal goal-scoring partnership with Jack Balmer, who refused to be overawed by the arrival of his expensive partner from St James's Park. Balmer achieved the distinction of scoring three hat-tricks in consecutive League games in 1946–47. The Reds charged up the table in the first half of the season, only to lose their momentum with some poor results around Christmas.

But with Balmer and Stubbins in prolific goal-scoring form – they cracked 48 goals between them that season – Liverpool raced to their fifth Championship.

That title-winning team contained one Bob Paisley, who was later to make more of a mark in management than he did in a long career as a player at Anfield.

Willie Fagan, a former Celtic and Preston player, captained the team, which combined strong defence with thrilling attack – set in motion more often than not by the still rapidly-improving Liddell.

First Wembley Final

Liddell, who went on to make a record number of appearances for the club, relied on strength, pace and awesome shooting power to become a nightmare for most First Division defences.

25 victories in 42 League games clinched the title. The squad was: Sidlow, Lambert, Spicer, Taylor, Hughes, Jones, Paisley, Priday, Balmer, Stubbins, Fagan (captain), Liddell, and Done.

Liverpool were unable to maintain the consistency that would later become a hallmark of their play. They dropped back into mid-table in 1947–8 and 1948–9, while Arsenal and Manchester United began to emerge as powerful post-War teams. Liverpool were still lurking in mid-table at the end of the 1949–50 season after a 19 match undefeated run at the beginning of the campaign had convinced their supporters that the title was theirs.

But as their League form rapidly deteriorated after Christmas, they began an F.A. Cup run that carried them to their first Wembley Final.

It took them two matches to dispose of Blackburn in the Third Round; poor Exeter City were crushed at Anfield; and Stockport County were beaten 2–1.

Now Billy Liddell took charge, scoring a late

goal to destroy a powerful Blackpool team in the quarter-finals.

Meanwhile, Everton were matching Liverpool's Cup form, with the prospect of an all-Mersey Final beginning to excite the city. The draw for the semi-finals foiled that hope with the two clubs coming out of the hat together for a clash at Maine Road.

Bob Paisley set the game alight before a gate of 73,000 by lobbing Everton's goalkeeper with a finely judged shot. Before Everton could recover, Liddell had squeezed a shot into their net from close range.

Laurie Hughes had recovered from injury to be considered for the Cup Final line-up against Arsenal. He duly returned and Paisley had the misfortune to be dropped, a decision he admitted later was the worst moment of his life.

Captained by Phil Taylor, who later became manager, Liverpool were 1–0 down in 15 minutes and despite gallant raids by Stubbins and Liddell were soundly beaten 2–0. F.A. Secretary Stanley Rous described it as the best footballing Final he had seen.

The Liverpool team at Wembley was: Sidlow, Lambert, Spicer, Taylor (captain), Hughes, Jones, Payne, Baron, Stubbins, Fagan, and Liddell.

Relegation

The 1950–51 season was notable only for the departure of manager George Kay after 15 years at the helm. Ill health forced him to retire and Don Welsh, a popular figure at Anfield in wartime games but better known for his exploits for Charlton and England, took over the reins.

Third Division Norwich ended Liverpool's dreams of returning to Wembley the following season. Despite huge post-War crowds, the club was making no impact in the early fifties under Welsh.

Their relegation to the Second Division, after being bottom club in the First in the 1953–54 season, interrupted an unbroken sequence of First Division status going back 50 years. Relegation cost Welsh his job, and in leaving Anfield he became the only manager ever to be sacked by Liverpool.

Life in the Second Division

Phil Taylor, a powerful half-back who had joined the club in 1936 and captained the Cup Final team, stepped enthusiastically into the void left by Welsh.

A popular figure, he commanded the respect of Liddell and Hughes, the only survivors of the great post-War team. He also had eager support from a crop of young players making their mark with the club in unfamiliar Second Division territory.

Life in the Second Division did nothing to damage the Kop's fervour for cheering their favourites. Tommy Younger maintained Liverpool's tradition for fielding fine goalkeepers. An agile and athletic Scot, he appeared in European competition for his former club Hibernian, thus becoming Liverpool's first Euro performer.

Jimmy Melia, an inside forward groomed from reserve ranks, was a magnificent servant in more than 250 appearances. Geoff Twentyman, signed from Carlisle United, was a formidable wing-half. Ronnie Moran, now one of Liverpool's bootroom generals, wore the number three shirt in almost 350 appearances for the club from 1952–64. Alan A'Court, who understudied Liddell in his early career at Anfield, broke through to win the first of five England caps in 1958 and go on to make 354 appearances for Liverpool.

A champion among champions

All these career records of longevity hardly measured up to Billy Liddell's proud career span. He wore the Liverpool shirt on 492 occasions in all, and scored 216 goals. In 1947 his remarkable contribution to Liverpool's success in winning the Championship was marked by his appearance in a Great Britain team against the Rest of Europe.

Liddell spent more than half his Liverpool career in the Second Division, yet exile from the top flight did nothing to dent his popularity or his capacity to enjoy an outstanding international career with Scotland.

When manager Phil Taylor resigned after a dismal start to the 1959–60 campaign, Liddell was tipped for possible promotion to the hot-seat.

Bob Paisley was said to be another candidate, but the job of steering Liverpool from the mediocrity of Second Division life was given to a 46-year-old Scot by the name of Bill Shankly. They didn't know it then, but life at Liverpool would never be quite the same after Shankly's arrival from his management post at Huddersfield Town.

Chapter Three

Enter Emperor Shankly

BILL SHANKLY'S arrival lit the flame that continues to blaze fiercely over Anfield, Liverpool 4, to this day.

The Reds were an unambitious, struggling Second Division outfit when Shankly breezed into Anfield on Tuesday, 1 December, 1959. Over the next 15 years his dare-devil drive and football brains would turn Liverpool from also-rans into one of the world's most powerful and respected club sides.

Born in Scotland near Ayr racecourse in 1913, Shankly was one of 10 children. His five brothers all played professional football. Anticipating a life of toil down the mines, Shankly never quite recovered from the shock moment when a Carlisle United official said they were prepared to *pay* him for playing a game he loved playing for nothing!

Shankly made his name as a hard tackling wing-half at Preston North End from 1933, winning an F.A. Cup winners' medal in 1938 before making the first of five appearances for his beloved Scotland.

Bill Shankly – determined to restore Liverpool to greatness.

His passion for football was unrivalled. He was made for the game – and for Liverpool. He was highly opinionated in his early managerial career at Carlisle and later at Huddersfield, but his red-blooded comments on football as manager of Liverpool were to be much repeated, and he was much loved. He told his players they were the greatest in the world. More importantly, they believed they were the greatest.

Former England captain Kevin Keegan, one of Shankly's greatest-ever signings, once said: 'I would run through a brick wall for that man.'

Soon after his arrival at Anfield, Shanks went into a hairdresser's in Liverpool. 'The usual Mr Shankly, short back and sides . . . and plenty off the top?' enquired the barber. 'Aye, Everton,' snapped Shanks.

His feverish commitment to the development of Liverpool rubbed off on the entire playing and backroom staff at Anfield.

He once caught a young apprentice drinking water from a tap at the training ground. 'Nay lad, don't drink that. Come with me and drink Anfield water.'

It was Shanks who inspired a sign-writer to paint a notice on the tunnel leading to the pitch. 'This is Anfield' says the sign, a statement that was soon to drive fear into most League opponents visiting the Liverpool stronghold.

A clean sweep
Shankly's first task after joining the Reds was to draw up a blueprint for scouting, coaching, training and playing that is as fresh and as sensible today as it was in his first few months at Anfield.

On fitness, he said: 'You can get so fit that you are almost immune from injuries – like a rubber ball.'

If he saw a young professional showing less than total commitment in training, he would tell him: 'I was not satisfied unless I could sprint for 90 minutes, let alone play for 90 minutes.'

He was under no false illusions about the size of the job he had undertaken on arrival from Huddersfield. 'The ground was an eyesore. It needed renovating and cleaning up. It was not good enough for the public of Liverpool and the team was not good enough for the public of Liverpool.'

Shankly's team

Shankly drew up a list of 24 players who were not part of his plans. Within a year, all 24 had been ruthlessly dispatched to other clubs.

A young centre-forward named Roger Hunt was one of the few players to survive Shankly's purge. Even in those early months of his reign, Shankly's perception was spot-on. Hunt scored 21 goals as Liverpool finished third in Division Two at the end of the 1959–60 season.

A 17-year-old fresh-faced Ian Callaghan was plucked from the youth team for a run in the Second Division side. He was to remain ever-present for the next two decades.

Shankly's first major signing was Gordon Milne, a key member of Preston's midfield whom Shankly had known since boyhood. And Gerry Byrne, who had been languishing in the reserves with little hope of displacing left-back Ronnie

Moran, was handed the number three shirt with Moran moving to right-back.

Everton's free-scoring striker Dave Hickson arrived and Kevin Lewis, Sheffield United's small winger with an unerring eye for the target, moved to Anfield. But the restless manager was not making the initial impact he wanted.

Once again Liverpool were to finish third in the Second Division as the 1960–61 season closed with fans beginning to turn their back on the club they had followed so enthusiastically in the golden Championship year after the War.

The summer of 1961 was to bring a significant turning point in Liverpool's fortunes. It happened when Shankly plunged into the transfer market to sign Ian St John from Motherwell for £37,000, and Ron Yeats from Dundee United for £30,000.

Shankly had indulged in a great deal of arm-twisting to persuade a sceptical board of directors that if Liverpool wanted the best team in the world, they had better sign good players.

Within a few days St John had silenced the critics. He scored a hat-trick in his début against Everton.

Liverpool took the Second Division by storm, losing only seven League games in cracking 99 goals. They clinched the title – and promotion – on 21 April 1962 when they beat Southampton before a 40,000 Anfield crowd.

Football fever

Across the city pop mania had arrived. The Beatles were beginning to 'yeah, yeah, yeah' their way to international fame. A music and football revolution had started on Merseyside, and the Kop caught the fever with their 'Liv-er-pool, Liv-er-pool, Liv-er-pool' chant.

Ron Yeats, dubbed the 'Red Colossus', was given the job of captaining Liverpool in their first season back in the First Division after an eight year absence. Standing 6ft 2ins and weighing 14 stone, the giant Scot was to command Liverpool defences for the next decade. His team made steady progress in the League, but their F.A. Cup campaign was spectacular.

Wrexham, Burnley, Arsenal and West Ham were all crushed by the new Liverpool machine; but Leicester, their semi-final opponents, were to prove a final stumbling block. The great England goalkeeper Gordon Banks was equal to everything Roger Hunt and the rest could hurl at him.

Liverpool finished eighth in the League with Hunt and St John scoring 43 goals between them. More significantly, a defence that had leaked badly in previous seasons was beginning to look as safe as a bank vault.

This was due largely to the arrival of Tommy Lawrence, who had looked a no-hoper at Anfield until Shankly inspired the young goalkeeper to believe in himself. Such was his progress that season that Scotland pressed him into service.

Liverpool had six internationals in their ranks by the end of 1962–63: Lawrence, Milne, Hunt, Byrne, Melia and A'Court.

From the day of his arrival Shankly had preached the importance of winning the League Championship. 'The Cup is a bonus, the Championship is our target,' he stressed.

Peter Thompson, a club record £40,000

signing from Preston, was to prove the difference between a mid-table berth for Liverpool and the ultimate prize at the end of the 1963–64 season. The older faction of Liverpool's enormous crowds called Thompson the new Billy Liddell. His wing wizardry, involving long mazy runs at high speed to the corner flag, reminded so many of the legendary Scot's touchline devilry of the immediate post-War era.

It certainly added a new dimension to Liverpool's play as they powered above Manchester United, continuing rivals Everton, and the big London clubs to clinch their sixth Championship.

Koppites talk about Thompson's double strike in that season's 5-0 defeat of Arsenal even today, but Roger Hunt, now firmly installed in an England shirt, did most of the season's damage, scoring 31 League goals.

The Cup Final
The next two years were to confirm the success of the blueprint Shankly had drawn up at the beginning of his reign.

The Reds' failure to slip smoothly into gear at the start of the 1964–65 season cost them their title but such was their strength and belief in themselves that if one trophy eluded them, they could seize on the probability of winning another.

This time they became Cup-fighting tigers. West Bromwich Albion, Stockport County (after a replay), Bolton, and Liverpool's bogey team Leicester, were gunned down as Shankly's men raced into the F.A. Cup semi-finals for a meeting with Chelsea.

The rivalry between Chelsea and Liverpool was

increased by the matching of Shankly against his former Preston team-mate Tommy Docherty, then in charge at Stamford Bridge.

A crowd of almost 68,000 saw Liverpool storm through to the Wembley Final in a 2-0 victory with goals by Willie Stevenson (penalty) and Peter Thompson.

Neither Liverpool nor their Final opponents Leeds United had ever won the Cup when they met at Wembley in what promised to be a classic.

All the optimism faded as a 100,000 crowd were forced to endure a goalless first 90 minutes, the first time a Cup Final had gone to extra-time since 1947.

Three minutes into extra-time Thompson slipped the ball to Gerry Byrne who crossed for Roger Hunt to break the deadlock. Billy Bremner equalised with Leeds' only shot of the match, but the ill-luck that had dogged Liverpool's Cup campaigns for more than 70 years was swept into oblivion when Ian Callaghan set up Ian St John for an explosive header to clinch a famous 2-0 victory.

Ron Yeats lifted the trophy, the Kop was in full voice, and manager Shankly revealed a secret. He disclosed that full-back Gerry Byrne had broken his collarbone in a collision with Bobby Collins after only three minutes of play. In those days before substitutes, Byrne had pleaded to stay on the pitch and went on to produce the bravest performance by any Liverpool player in the club's long and proud history.

City chiefs reckon that half a million people lined the streets of Liverpool when the Reds returned home on the Sunday.

The World Cup

The momentum of Liverpool's two trophy winning seasons was maintained in the 1965–66 season. 'The Championship, then the F.A. Cup, how can they follow that?' argued the faint-hearted.

They need hardly have worried as Roger Hunt struck the form that was to carry him to World Cup triumph in the summer of 1966. He ended the season with 30 League goals, the fifth successive season he had headed Liverpool's marksmen.

Liverpool had clinched the League title by a handsome six point margin from Leeds United. Three Liverpool heroes, Roger Hunt, Ian Callaghan and Gerry Byrne, were then invited to join England's World Cup squad by Alf Ramsey.

Six years after his arrival on a £2500 salary, Bill Shankly was undisputed King of the Kop, and Liverpool Football Club's most priceless asset.

Chapter Four

You'll Never Walk Alone

The Kop's ear-splitting victory chant of 'ee-aye-adio' inspired all soccer supporters to develop their own songs in the pop crazy days of the 1960s.

Liverpool's fans went a stage further than simply producing a few catch-phrases. They borrowed a song from 'Gerry and the Pacemakers', a favourite group from Merseyside, which became their anthem on the long journeys into Europe that became the fashion for the trophy-winning Reds. The Kop adopted Gerry's moving version of 'You'll Never Walk Alone' on a series of European crusades that followed Liverpool's European Cup entry following their Championship win in 1963–64.

Into Europe
Manchester United had reached the European Cup semi-finals in 1957 and 1958; but once the Busby Babes had perished at Munich, English clubs had made no impact on foreign soil.

Liverpool launched their first European campaign in August 1964 when they pumped 11 goals into Reykjavik's net over their two encounters. A young Tommy Smith was drafted into the team to take on Belgian champions Anderlecht. They cruised to a handsome 3-0 advantage at Anfield and stunned a 50,000 Anderlecht gate by winning the second leg 1-0.

It took Liverpool 300 minutes to overcome Cologne and become only the second English team to reach the European Cup semi-finals.

The result was decided on the toss of a coin after the two legs and a replay with extra time had ended all square. Even then the result was decided in bizarre fashion, the coin having to be tossed again after it had landed on its edge in thick mud.

The semi-final brought a head-on clash between Liverpool and Inter Milan – Champions of the World, Europe and Italy.

Anfield was jammed to the rafters and Shankly, warming to the occasion, played a managerial ace by parading before the fans the F.A. Cup Liverpool had just won. The stadium erupted when Gerry Byrne, nursing a broken collarbone, and Gordon Milne, carried the Cup towards the Kop. Inter Milan, kicking a ball about in their warm-up routine, wilted visibly in the face of the electric current Shankly's master-stroke had generated.

Despite their pedigree, Inter Milan were no match for Liverpool, who stormed into the second-leg with a 3-1 advantage on the strength of goals from Roger Hunt, Ian Callaghan and Ian St John. Inter's famous manager Helenio Herrara observed darkly: 'We have been beaten before. Tonight we were defeated.'

His misery was short-lived, however. In one of

Ian St John – Bill Shankly's first major signing.

the most controversial second-legs in European history, Inter reduced the deficit in just 20 minutes in the San Siro stadium and went on to reach the European Cup Final. *Sunday Times* investigators were to allege that the referee was bribed, a condemnation supported to the hilt by an angry and disappointed Bill Shankly.

More competition
Liverpool's 1965 F.A. Cup Final triumph entitled them to enter the European Cup-Winners' Cup for the first time and carry their Euro experience into another major continental competition.

Liverpool were trailing Italian giants Juventus by just one goal after a rugged first leg encounter in Turin. The chill of an October evening in 1965 was melted by a 51,000 strong Anfield gate who cheered the Reds to victory by courtesy of match-winning strikes by Chris Lawler, the most adventurous defender in the League, and former Arsenal star Geoff Strong.

Standard Liège, the Belgian Cup winners, were no match for Liverpool in the next round. They powered into the third round, for battle with the crack Hungarian Army team, Honved. The great Hungarian team of the 1950s had relied heavily on Honved players, Puskas, Kocsis, Czibor and Bozsik, to weave their magic across the world; but a decade later the pride of the mighty Magyars had wilted and Liverpool sailed into the semi-finals for a clash with Jock Stein's mighty Celtic.

A single strike by Bobby Lennox saw Celtic hold a slender 1-0 advantage from the first leg at Parkhead. The second leg provided another of those gripping 'European nights' at Anfield.

Celtic were clinging to their 1-0 lead at the interval, but the break Liverpool sought came on the hour as they piled on pressure in a series of feverish attacks towards the Kop end. Tommy Smith, the lionheart of Liverpool's midfield, squared the game when he drove a fierce free-kick through Celtic's defensive wall from outside the penalty box.

Five minutes later Liverpool's passage to their first European Final was sealed when Geoff Strong, so often a saviour of lost causes, shrugged off the pain of a torn cartilage to head Ian Callaghan's cross into Celtic's net.

A Bobby Lennox goal was ruled off-side just before the end, and the game ended in mayhem with Celtic fans sending a fusillade of bottles onto the pitch in their disgust.

Stormy weather

Liverpool fought the European Cup-Winners' Cup Final against Borussia Dortmund in a rain-ravaged Hampden Park. Only 41,000 tickets were sold and Liverpool never looked like winning.

Borussia's first half goal was cancelled out by Roger Hunt, but with just seconds of the match remaining the England striker missed a sitter that was to haunt him for years. Borussia won in extra-time, but with Liverpool's League win in 1965–66, they could look forward to another European Cup campaign in 1966–67.

The Kop reserved a special welcome for their ace marksman Roger Hunt at the start of the 1966–67 season. He had played in all six of England's World Cup winning matches and the great Liverpool servant was given a huge cheer when he stepped out at Goodison with his England team-mates, Alan Ball and Ray Wilson, both of Everton. They paraded the World Cup, the Championship trophy and the F.A. Cup to the massed ranks of Merseyide fans before the Charity Shield match against Everton.

Liverpool's third European campaign started unconvincingly with a narrow victory over Rumanian champions Petrolul Ploetsi. The next round, against crack Dutch club Ajax, was to demonstrate to Bill Shankly that his team was not as good as he thought it was. Maybe he needed to re-build if he wanted to win another League title and enjoy success in Europe.

The first leg was played in a fog-bound Olympic stadium in Amsterdam. It was impossible to see from one end of the pitch to the other, but the conditions clearly suited Ajax who romped to a 5-1 first leg victory.

Ajax forced a 2-2 draw in the return and the Kop gave a moving salute to the Dutch side, in particular a young forward by the name of Johan Cruyff, who in later years would terrorise World Cup defences.

Time for change
Liverpool's humiliating performance forced Shankly into the transfer market. A cheque for £65,000 persuaded Blackpool to part with Emlyn Hughes, a Barrow-born all-action player who was to become one of the Red's most versatile players and a Kop favourite.

Born on 28 August 1987, Hughes was christened 'Crazy Horse'; a tribute to his wild, forward gallops from defence into attack. He went on to make 474 League appearances over the next 12 years. As captain, he saw Liverpool through to three League titles in four years, to F.A. Cup Final triumphs, and to success in Europe.

Tony Hateley arrived from Chelsea for a club record fee of £96,000, and for just £18,000 Shankly grabbed Scunthorpe's goalkeeper Ray Clemence.

The chopping and changing continued as loyal servants Gordon Milne and Willie Stevenson were off-loaded at the end of distinguished careers at Anfield.

Liverpool's fifth position in the League in 1966–67 entitled them to enter the European Fairs Cup. Tony Hateley scored two scorching goals to polish off Malmo in the first leg, and Ron Yeats and Roger Hunt completed the demolition at Anfield.

Munich were touched 8-0; but Liverpool's European campaign was ended dramatically by Hungarian club Ferencvaros, who became the first foreign club to win at Anfield.

Despite all the unfulfilled promise in Europe, the full thunder of 'You'll Never Walk Alone' had still to be heard. The Kop were right behind Shankly as he strove to find the right team combination for a successful assault on the domestic competitions which would guarantee entry to Europe – now an essential part of any winter campaign.

New-look Reds
Liverpool managed to make only the European Fairs Cup grade between 1967–68 and 1970–71. These were fairly barren years by Shankly's standards.

Ray Clemence replaced Tommy Lawrence, a veteran of more than 300 appearances in the Liverpool jersey. Ron Yeats, Ian St John and Roger Hunt, the backbone of his first, great Liverpool team, were banished from the first team in 1969–70 and such names as Alun Evans, Alec Lindsay, and Larry Lloyd, a powerful centre-half from Bristol Rovers, began to receive the hero-worship of an increasingly restless and despondent Kop.

By the end of the 1970–71 season Shankly had cut the average age of his team to 22. Trophies were still eluding them but there was increasing evidence of a new Liverpool. The team began to shape up, blending all the cut and thrust of Shankly's glory team of the early days, with the skill and enterprise that 'boot room' staff Bob Paisley, Ronnie Moran and Joe Fagan had driven into the squad.

Steve Heighway, born in Dublin on 25 November 1947, arrived clutching a BA from Warwick University and a proud record of wing wizardry as an amateur for Skelmersdale.

He joined Brian Hall, a graduate of Manchester University who had been on Liverpool's books for a couple of years. John Toshack, a tall, willowy striker from Cardiff was picked up for £110,000. He had scored 74 goals in 161 League games for the Welsh club, a strike rate he repeated in almost the same number of appearances for Liverpool over the next seven years.

Liverpool were to finish fifth behind the champions Arsenal at the end of the 1970–71 campaign; but the new-look Reds were beginning to make their mark again against the crack European teams.

Full season

Liverpool avenged that Anfield defeat by Ferencvaros in the Fairs Cup. Dynamo Bucharest were overwhelmed and the Scottish League side Hibernian felt Toshack's sting on his European début when his goal divided the teams in the first leg in Edinburgh.

Victory at Anfield in the second leg was a formality, achieved through goals from Phil Boersma and Heighway, whose thrilling touchline runs were giving First Division right-backs nightmares in his first season.

Bayern Munich, the Bundesliga Champions, were next to cower before Liverpool's European anthem inspired by 'Gerry and the Pacemakers'. They paraded half the German team, including Sepp Maier, Georg Schwarzenbeck, Franz Beckenbauer (who had masterminded England's World Cup quarter-final exit in 1970), Gerd Muller and Uli Hoeness. Alun Evans, a temperamental star whose attitude was to cut his Liverpool career short, produced his finest performance for the Reds. He gunned a hat-trick past Maier in one of the best games seen at Anfield for many years.

Liverpool surged into the semi-final, after forcing a draw in Munich, only to run up against

Revie's powerful Leeds United team. Leeds scored the only goal in two legs and Liverpool had failed in Europe again.

Such was Liverpool's strength and interest in all competitions that if they failed in one contest, they often surged through in another. Their 1970-71 campaign was to end with a Wembley appearance in the 1971 F.A. Cup Final.

They faced Arsenal in a repeat of the 1950 Final, and nothing could deny the Gunners from becoming the second club to complete the magic League and Cup double.

With no score at full-time, the Final drifted into extra-time, which was far more dramatic than the first 90 minutes. Steve Heighway went past two Arsenal defenders to shoot Liverpool ahead. Bob Wilson saved instinctively from Brian Hall to keep Arsenal in the game, then goals by Eddie Kelly and Charlie George destroyed Liverpool's dream.

Fifth in the League, runners-up in Europe, beaten at Wembley: Liverpool had no cause to be too upset in a season that had embraced 62 matches.

Keegan on the scene

Sitting in the Wembley stands was a 20-year-old by the name of Kevin Keegan. Shankly had snapped him up from Scunthorpe United for a mere £35,000.

The next time Liverpool appeared at Wembley, Keegan would be in the team – and they would *not* lose.

Kevin Keegan, born in Armthorpe, Yorkshire on 14 February 1951, made his First Division

Kevin Keegan, who scored 68 goals in 230 games for Liverpool.

début in Liverpool's opening game of the 1971–72 season. Over the next decade he was to turn himself into a world-class player and a veteran of 63 England appearances. Jimmy Greaves, a former England striker and ardent supporter of Keegan's, paid this tribute: 'I always admired Kevin's great industry. There were more skilful and more inventive players, but his remarkable work rate when coupled with his considerable ability lifted him above most of his rivals.'

Keegan was built like a pocket battleship. Only 5ft 8ins tall, he showed in those early appearances for Liverpool that he could out-jump and out-smart most First Division defences. He was strong, could ride the fiercest tackles, and if he caught sight of goal he was always likely to score.

His partnership with Toshack wrecked not only First Division defences but terrorised some of the strongest rearguards in Europe. Could it be that this new formation, spearheaded by Toshack and Keegan, could clinch Shankly's first European trophy?

Top form
Leeds knocked Liverpool out of the F.A. Cup; Bayern Munich halted their progress in the European Cup-Winners' Cup; and in a cliff-hanging finale to the Championship, a Toshack 'goal' against Arsenal was disallowed and they had to be content with third place in the First Division.

A fee of £100,000 captured Peter Cormack from Nottingham Forest to inject fresh interest in the team for the start of the 1972–73 season.

Clemence, Lawler, Smith, Lloyd, Hughes, Callaghan, Heighway and Toshack were all established internationals at one level or other. Shankly was forging the nucleus of another great Liverpool side. The club surged to its eighth First Division title and was beginning to make its mark across the length and breadth of the football-playing Continent. Eintracht Frankfurt, AEK Athens, Dynamo Berlin and Dynamo Dresden were all swept aside as the Reds stampeded into the semi-finals of the UEFA Cup (the former Fairs Cup).

Liverpool faced the mighty Spurs, winners of the UEFA Cup the previous season, in a two-leg semi-final. A solitary goal by Liverpool defender Alec Lindsay split the sides at Anfield, but two goals by Martin Peters, with a reply by Heighway, gave Spurs a 2-1 victory at White Hart Lane. As Heighway's away goal counted double, Liverpool were through to a two-leg Final against the masterful Borussia Moenchengladbach, rated the best team in Europe by Shankly.

The referee called off the first leg at Anfield after just half an hour, played in torrential rain. Shankly's brief glimpse of the Germans convinced him that their defence was leaden footed and weak in the air.

Shanks changed his line-up for the re-convened meeting the following night, replacing Brian Hall with John Toshack. Rarely had his judgment been better, for Toshack's height caused chaos, enabling Kevin Keegan to score twice, and centre-half Larry Lloyd to weigh in with another goal in a thrilling 3-0 victory.

Liverpool weathered an onslaught to clinch the trophy on a 3-2 aggregate in the second leg. In playing 64 games that season, they had become

Above: **Payne (behind No 7) fails to score in the 1950 F.A. Cup Final.**

Above: **Stubbins playing centre for Liverpool at Highbury, 1949.**

Above: **Tommy Smith and Ian Callaghan (in the Hat) hold up the European Cup after victory in 1977.**

Left: **Bob Paisley with the League Championship Trophy in 1983.**

Above: **The Bill Shankly Memorial Gates at Anfield.**

Above: **Bill Shankly greets the Kop.**

Above: **The European Cup again – in 1984, held by Robinson (left) and Grobbelaar.**

Above: **Kenny Dalglish in the 1986 F.A. Cup Final against Everton.**

Above: **Liverpool bring home the 'Double', 1986.**

Above: **1987–8 League Champions. Back, L to R: Dalglish (manager), Evans (trainer), Macdonald, Venison, Molby, Whelan, Hooper, Barnes, Johnson, Spackman, Gillespie, Grobbelaar, Moran (coach). Front, L to R: Beglin, Aldridge, McMahon, Beardsley, Hansen, Nicol, Houghton, Ablett.**

Above: **Kevin Keegan challenges Alan Mullery of Spurs.**

Above: **Ian Rush goes for the ball.**

Above: **John Barnes weaves between the opposition.**

Above: **Mark Lawrenson tries hard to get the ball from Adrian Heath of Everton!**

Right: **Peter Beardsley, always determined, in the 1988 F.A. Cup semi-final against Nottingham Forest.**

the first Football League club to lift the Championship and a major European trophy.

No player had done more for the team than Keegan, who had bagged 22 goals – five more than his attacking sidekick Toshack.

Keeping up the act
The 1973–74 season was to see Liverpool trail Leeds United in First Division and fail miserably to emulate their European form of the previous season. They crashed out of the European Cup to Red Star Belgrade.

They still could not get their act together in the League Cup, which in those days was still not truly accepted by the big clubs as a major competition.

Their only hope was in the F.A. Cup, and they duly appeared in their fifth Final after John Toshack had performed wonders in earlier rounds.

They faced Newcastle United in the 1974 Cup Final, with the Magpies tipped to give Liverpool a torrid time. Their England striker, Malcolm Macdonald, known as 'Supermac' at St James's Park, had been cruelly tagged 'Supermouth' by the Kop on account of his boastful utterances in the build-up.

It was not a contest! Newcastle were outplayed in the second half, and a double strike by Kevin Keegan, followed by a slick move by Toshack ending in Heighway's goal, gave Liverpool a 3-0 victory.

One of their heroes that day was 20-year-old Liverpool-born Phil Thompson, who had taken over from the injured Larry Lloyd at the heart of

Liverpool's defence, and hardly gave Macdonald and John Tudor a kick.

Thompson's face was so unfamiliar that a security guard tried to stop him climbing the steps to the Royal Box to receive his winner's medal.

Meanwhile, Bill Shankly was holding court in the stadium. 'This is the best team in England and probably the world,' he insisted.

Unwelcome news

The half million Liverpool supporters who lined the street of the great Northern city to welcome the team home were not to know it at the time, but it was their last opportunity to cheer Bill Shankly as the Reds' manager.

The Northern Press corps gathered at Anfield on 12 July 1974 to learn that Ray Kennedy had been signed from Arsenal for £200,000. And they learned something else from Liverpool's chairman John Smith in a terse statement: 'It is with great regret that as chairman of the board I have to inform you that Mr Shankly has intimated to us that he wishes to retire from League football.'

For the first time in Shanks' 15 year reign there was silence at Anfield!

Chapter Five

Paisley's Pirates Run Riot

SIR MATT BUSBY, Manchester United's greatest post-War manager, paid Bill Shankly the ultimate tribute. He said: 'As a young player, as an experienced international, as a young manager, as an experienced manager, his drive and enthusiasm never diminished. His marriage to the game has been the greatest love-match in its history.'

Shankly had become a legend in his own lifetime, spoken of and described in print for evermore as 'the legendary Bill Shankly'.

Critics searching for a crack in the seemingly impregnable fabric of Liverpool Football Club were saying knowingly: 'Follow that.' The thrust of their argument was that no living being could slip comfortably into Shankly's seat at Anfield and emulate the astonishing feats of the Great Man.

They were wrong.

Paisley days
Shankly's successor emerged in the stocky shape of Bob Paisley, a shy, modest, quietly spoken man

born in the football-daft village of Hetton-le-Hole, Durham. Liverpool had spotted him playing for the famous amateur club Bishop Auckland and at 19 he became a professional at Anfield. A strong and clever half-back, he made 278 appearances for the Reds before donning a tracksuit to become a valuable member of that elite corps of 'boot room' boys.

The dial-a-quote days of Shankly had given way to the Paisley era in which he preferred to 'let my team do the talking'.

Liverpool's record under Paisley from the summer of 1974 until his retirement in June 1983 was staggering. They were League Champions in 1976, 1977, 1979, 1980, 1982 and 1983; League Milk Cup winners in 1981, 1982, and 1983; European Cup winners in 1977, 1978 and 1981; UEFA Cup winners in 1976; and F.A. Cup runners-up in 1977.

Paisley launched his managerial career impressively with Liverpool enjoying an unbeaten run of seven games. And in his first taste of European football, Stromgodset from Norway were put to the sword, and thrashed 11-0 at Anfield in the first round of the European Cup-Winners' Cup.

Sadly, Liverpool went out to old rivals Ferencvaros in the second round, and were shot out of the League Cup and F.A. Cup in double quick time. They remained in the hunt for the First Division title only to finish second best to Derby County.

Bob Paisley, who followed Bill Shankly as manager and was equally successful.

Transfer time
Paisley proved a shrewd bargain hunter in the transfer market. He signed Phil Neal from Northampton Town for just £60,000, a pittance for a player who went on to make more appearances at right-back for England than any other player.

Neal arrived in November 1974. One month later Terry McDermott, a restless, skilful midfield star at Newcastle United, was signed. A Mersey boy, he had escaped the scouting net to make his mark with Bury before moving to St James's Park.

Chris Lawler and Larry Lloyd were on the way out, and Ray Kennedy, signed from Arsenal, was struggling to establish himself in attack. Paisley revived the youngster's flagging career by forcing him to shed weight for a midfield role that was to establish him as one of the finest playmakers in the First Division.

Paisley's second season in charge served to silence the fast-diminishing band of critics who insisted that Liverpool would never recover from Shankly's departure.

Second season successes
The club made a modest start to the Championship battle, only to wind up the season in sensational fashion by turning a 1–0 deficit against Wolves into a 3–1 victory which carried them to the title. Kevin Keegan, John Toshack and Ray Kennedy scored the goals. Toshack and Keegan completed a combined tally of 28 goals that season! Three youngsters had played a major part in the campaign: Joey Jones, a £110,000 buy from Wrexham; Jimmy Case, promoted from the

reserves; and David Fairclough, the lad they called 'Supersub', in tribute to his lightning strikes in the number 12 shirt.

All the promise Liverpool had shown in European competition in the Shankly era was now beginning to blossom. Toshack, now at the peak of his goal-scoring powers, scored a hat-trick to demolish Hibernian's resistance in the first round of the UEFA Cup in 1975–76. Real Sociedad of Spain and Poland's Slask Wroclaw perished, and Dynamo Dresden were overcome in the quarter-finals.

To reach the Final Liverpool had to overcome Barcelona, the crack Spanish team containing Dutch stars Johan Neeskins and Johan Cruyff. Toshack's solitary strike clinched victory in the Nou Camp stadium and Liverpool reached the Final by holding Barcelona to a 1–1 draw at Anfield.

Bruges shook a 50,000 Anfield crowd by scorching into a 2–0 lead by the interval, but they were outmanoeuvred by Paisley's cunning deployment of Jimmy Case in Toshack's central striking position in the second half, to give Liverpool a 3–2 victory.

Kennedy, Case and Keegan had forged the one goal advantage for the second leg in Belgium but that was soon cancelled out when Bruges took an early lead from a penalty. Keegan then proved his worth, scoring one of the most important goals he managed in his six year career at Anfield.

Liverpool had completed the League and UEFA Double for the second time.

The arrival of £200,000 Ipswich striker David Johnson was not greeted with unanimous approval. He took several months to establish himself on his native Merseyside, but Paisley saw him as one for the future.

The most exciting game
Liverpool were protecting a secret at this time. Keegan, a Messiah on Merseyside, had expressed a wish to play on the continent; a request that Liverpool had granted on condition that he remain in their colours for one more season.

Paisley's target in 1976–77 was the European Cup, the premier prize that had proved beyond the reach of even Bill Shankly.

But first they blazed a thunderous trail in First Division action, losing only two of their first 16 games to head the table. They went on to become the first club to retain the Championship since Wolverhampton Wanderers back in the 1950s.

As always Anfield was an impregnable fortress, Liverpool winning 18 and drawing three of their League matches. They were less impressive away, winning only five League games, but they piled up enough points to outstrip Manchester City in the battle for the title. That renowned double-act of Keegan and Toshack did most of the damage. Kevin scored 13 League goals in his final season and Toshack weighed in with 11.

Liverpool moved into the last stages of the season on the crest of a remarkable treble. They had survived a semi-final replay with Everton to reach the F.A. Cup Final. They had destroyed Belfast Crusaders, Turkish champions Trabzonspor, French giants St Etienne, and Zurich of Switzerland en route to a European Cup Final clash with West Germany's Borussia Moenchengladbach.

They were also favourites for the First Division crown.

Liverpool's victory over St Etienne was one of the most exciting duels in the Reds' illustrious history. Trailing 1–0 after the first leg, Liverpool levelled the scores through Keegan within two minutes of the start of the second leg.

The teams were given a standing ovation at half-time; but just when Liverpool's confidence of victory was growing, Bathenay had equalised to put Liverpool back where they started.

Ray Kennedy's second-half goal relieved the pressure as they still trailed to the French away goal with Toshack now limping. Enter 'Supersub' Fairclough to produce the most stunning performance of his life. He skipped past two flat-footed St Etienne defenders on a devastating 40 yard run, and crashed the ball into the Frenchmen's net with just eight minutes left!

Emlyn Hughes rated that game the most exciting of his career. In more than 150 appearances for Liverpool, Fairclough was never to produce a finer performance.

Disaster strikes
The First Division title was wrapped up before the club took on Manchester United in the 1977 F.A. Cup Final, and Borussia in the European Cup Final.

Rarely had a Wembley occasion held more promise. Tommy Docherty's United were back at Wembley just one year after the shock of losing to Second Division Southampton; Liverpool were going for the treble.

In this game Fairclough was not even named

as substitute: Paisley preferred his new signing David Johnson to replace the injured Toshack. Kevin Keegan and Ray Kennedy foraged enthusiastically to give Liverpool midfield supremacy, but Johnson could not capitalise on the service.

Five minutes after half-time United's Stuart Pearson shook the ultra-reliable England goalkeeper Ray Clemence with a snap shot; but with perfect timing Jimmy Case dispatched a rocket drive beyond Alex Stepney for the equaliser.

The match ended in disaster for Paisley's men. Lou Macari's shot deflected off Jimmy Greenhoff's body and looped into Liverpool's net for the winner.

The League and Cup Double dream was shattered, and all hopes for the treble were lost.

Keegan's swan song

Five days later Liverpool emerged from the tunnel in Rome's Olympic stadium to receive a rapturous welcome from the 30,000 Reds' fans who had driven, hitch-hiked and flown to Italy, many of them embarking on the long journey straight from Wembley.

Could Liverpool shake off the disappointment of their calamitous performance against Manchester United? Lining up against the German champions were: Clemence, Neal, Smith, Kennedy, Hughes, Jones, Keegan, Case, Heighway, Callaghan, McDermott.

Facing them was one of Europe's most powerful machines, which included such stars as Rainer Bonhof, Berti Vogts, Urlich Stielike, Jupp

Heynckes, Allan Simonsen and Herbert Wimmer.

The Liverpool fans were now acutely aware of a factor that might be significant. The secret was out of the bag: this was to be Kevin Keegan's last game for Liverpool.

The prospect of Liverpool becoming the first British club to lift the precious European crown for nine years inspired Keegan to produce one of the finest displays of his glittering career. Given a roving role and trailed by his 'watchdog' Vogts – one of Europe's most efficient destroyers – Keegan ran his German marker ragged, pulling him all over the Olympic stadium.

Liverpool led after 27 minutes through Terry McDermott from a Steve Heighway pass. Simonsen equalised and Ray Clemence's goal was under siege in the second half.

At this point Keegan began to buzz in an amazing exhibition of long distance running. Heighway forced a corner and Tommy Smith, making his 600th appearance, rose to head his first goal of the season.

The Keegan-Vogts contest was in full swing by now, but it went Kevin's way decisively when the German flattened him on a surging run into Borussia's penalty area.

Phil Neal, Paisley's first transfer buy, stepped up to make it 3–1 from a penalty. Liverpool were European champions! The dazzling display was watched by a five million strong television audience.

Bob Paisley had become the most celebrated club manager in the world. Sober too! He resisted the temptation to drink the victory champagne, saying 'I just wanted to savour the atmosphere.' He had never tried to step out of Shankly's shadow, but had happily succeeded.

Emlyn Hughes, the captain on that glorious night in Rome, observed less happily: 'I still curse the memory of that shot from Lou Macari that was missing the target until deflected into our net by Jimmy Greenhoff. But for that we might have had all three major trophies, which would have given us a unique place in history.'

Keegan reflected: 'The memory of that match when we won the European Cup will live with me forever.'

Fresh faces
Keegan's departure to Hamburg in a £500,000 deal in June 1977 upset the Kop. Some never forgave the England man. 'How can he leave the greatest club in the world?' they argued.

Keegan's ambition drove him out, so Liverpool needed to pull off one of their customary transfer swoops in mid-summer. True to form, Paisley managed the greatest transfer in Liverpool's history. For £440,000 he bagged 26-year-old Kenny Dalglish from Celtic. Kenny's record was unparalleled in the Scottish League – 112 goals in 204 League games, averaging a goal every other outing.

Tommy Smith was persuaded to drop his plans to leave Liverpool and a 22-year-old former Partick Thistle defender was being sharpened for First Division action in the reserves. His name? Alan Hansen.

By Liverpool standards their 1977–78 League

campaign was disappointing. They finished First Division runners-up behind Nottingham Forest.

They crashed out of the F.A. Cup, but their barren life in the League Cup competition blossomed into an all-out assault on the trophy. Chelsea, Derby, Coventry, Wrexham, and Arsenal were swept aside as Liverpool ploughed into the Final for a contest with Brian Clough's Nottingham Forest.

Former Liverpool star Larry Lloyd helped repel all Liverpool attacks in a dour Wembley struggle, and a replay was ordered at Old Trafford. Tragically, Phil Thompson's wild tackle on John O'Hare cost Liverpool a penalty and John Robertson broke the deadlock from the spot.

Television re-runs of the incident were to reveal that Thompson's tackle was outside the penalty area.

The new boys rule
Graeme Souness was beginning to make a major contribution to Liverpool's midfield following his £350,000 move from Middlesbrough in January 1978.

He was to play a leading part in Liverpool's romp to their second successive European Cup Final appearance. Dynamo Dresden, Benfica, and old foe Borussia Moenchengladbach were all beaten handsomely as the Reds won the right to play FC Bruges in the 1978 European Cup Final at Wembley.

Kenny Dalglish had more than adequately replaced the departed Keegan. His goal credit before Wembley was 29 strikes, each goal sending the Kop into raptures. 'Dal-glish, Dal-glish' was to become their favourite chant over the next decade.

New-boys Dalglish and Souness combined to unlock a formidable Bruges defence in a Final that was disappointing apart from the one goal scored. Graeme played a slide-rule pass to King Kenny, and in the true tradition of great strikers, the canny Scot coolly chipped past the advancing Jensen, enabling Liverpool to become the first British team to clinch the trophy in successive years.

Their glory boys on that day were: Clemence, Neal, Thompson, Hansen, Kennedy, Hughes, Dalglish, Case (Heighway), Fairclough, McDermott and Souness.

The next two seasons were to see Liverpool maintain their stranglehold on the First Division, and John Toshack and Emlyn Hughes depart from Anfield at the end of brilliant careers.

Toshack left to become player-manager of ambitious Swansea after scoring 74 goals in 172 games over seven years. Hughes, a veteran of 474 League games between 1966–78, had captained Liverpool to three League titles in four years, to UEFA Cup and FA Cup Final triumphs, and to the first two of the club's European Cup Final victories. He moved to Wolves, having repaid every penny of the record fee of £65,000 that Shankly had splashed out.

Unbeaten masters
By now Liverpool were the masters of the unbeaten-run. They lost only one League game from mid-December 1978, winning the title by eight points from Nottingham Forest. They remained

unbeaten from September to mid-January and retained their title in 1979–80.

Terry McDermott, the sharp-witted England midfield man, sparked Liverpool's tremendous run in the F.A. Cup in 1980. Having disposed of Grimsby, McDermott scored one of the goals that sank Nottingham Forest in the next round, and the little midfield general went on to hammer a scorching shot into Tottenham's net that saw the club into the semi-finals.

It took four games to sort out winners and losers in a series of stirring encounters between Liverpool and Arsenal, the Gunners finally taking the ultimate prize of an appearance in the Cup Final.

Johnson, now firmly established and confirming his potential, scored 27 goals that season, but who should be arriving through the front door at Anfield? Fresh from Fourth Division football at Chester City came Ian Rush, for £300,000. There was no limit to Paisley's acumen in the transfer business!

Third European Cup hopes
Liverpool were never in the hunt for the Championship in 1980–81. They even lost their unprecedented home record of unbeaten matches when they conceded defeat at Anfield to bogey team Leicester City after 85 games.

Everton shot them out of the F.A. Cup as the Reds embarked on a Milk Cup run that sent them soaring into a Wembley Final against West Ham.

Ray Kennedy's goal in the first leg, and Dalglish's solitary strike in the second, had seen off Manchester City in the semi-final.

Alan Kennedy, nicknamed 'Barney', went on one of his foraging runs to put Liverpool ahead at Wembley but with just 60 seconds remaining, West Ham equalised from a penalty and forced a replay.

This time Liverpool made no mistake. First Dalglish and then Hansen, making a major contribution in his first full season, shot the Reds to their first triumph in a competition that had long defeated them.

In the European Cup, Graeme Souness scored hat-tricks against Oulun Palloseura and CSKA Sofia to confirm his pedigree as one of Scotland's finest players. Liverpool were determined to win their third European Cup. They drew mighty Bayern Munich in the semi-finals, but after a goalless first-leg at Anfield had little hopes for the return. However, Howard Gayle enjoyed one of those performances that shatter the formbooks. He hardly got a mention in the match programme, but once he had skipped out of his tracksuit on the subs' bench he gave the Germans' defence a roasting.

Ray Kennedy put Liverpool ahead, Karl-Heinz Rummenigge equalised and the away goal advantage put Liverpool through to their third European Cup Final.

Mourning the Great Man
Liverpool, the new kings of Europe, were pitched against Real Madrid, the old masters of continental football who were making their ninth appearance in the Final. They had been winners six times!

It had all the makings of a blistering encounter

Graeme Souness (right), one of Bob Paisley's shrewdest signings.

65

in the Parcs des Princes stadium in Paris. But this time the build-up overshadowed performance in a surprisingly uneventful match.

Liverpool defender Alan Kennedy would disagree with that verdict, for it was he who strode on to Ray Kennedy's sharply taken throw to move in for the kill in the form of a thunderbolt shot past a demoralised Agustin.

Paisley's pirates had triumphed again. No man was more proud of Liverpool's achievements in Europe than Bill Shankly, now seven years into retirement.

Four months after watching Liverpool's latest Euro classic, Shanks was rushed to hospital. He died on 28 September 1981.

His beloved Kop didn't wear black. They mourned in red and white, standing silently on the Anfield terraces in a moving salute to the man who launched the Liverpool juggernaut on its rise from Second Division obscurity to European greatness.

Snap judgement

Liverpool's traditional plunge into the transfer market between seasons saw a departure in 1981. Ray Clemence, a veteran of 470 League appearances after making the same trek as Kevin Keegan from Scunthorpe to Anfield for a bargain £20,000, was sold sensationally to Spurs for £300,000.

Into the breach stepped a 24-year-old Bruce Grobbelaar. His transfer to Liverpool had taken less than a minute. Paisley travelled to Vancouver in March 1981 to watch Bruce play for the Whitecaps.

The interview was short even by Paisley's standards of measured and rationed conversation. 'Do you want to play for Liverpool?' 'Yes,' Bruce replied. 'That will do for me,' grinned Paisley.

Winning tactics

Liverpool stormed to yet another League Championship in 1981–82. They clinched the title on the strength of their dynamic spearhead involving Dalglish and new-boy Ian Rush, who smashed 17 League goals in his first season.

Craig Johnston had followed Souness from Middlesbrough to Merseyside in a £500,000 deal, but he would see his chances limited as Liverpool swept into gear for a second crack in successive years at winning the Milk Cup.

They made it to Wembley after a cliff-hanging two leg semi-final battle with Bobby Robson's Ipswich Town. Ian Rush and Terry McDermott scored the goals that divided the teams in the first leg, and Liverpool forced a 2–2 draw in the second.

Who should be facing Liverpool at Wembley? None other than Ray Clemence, who turned on a prodigious show of goalkeeping for a 100,000 crowd.

Steve Archibald put Spurs ahead and would have clinched the match with an 85th minute effort, had Souness not been alert enough to clear his line.

Liverpool piled on the pressure and with just two minutes left equalised through Ronnie Whelan, who had arrived from Irish club Home Farm for a small fee in April 1981.

Tottenham's weary players slumped to the turf

in the break before extra-time. Paisley, striding through his players, ordered them to skip around as if bouncing on springs in a clever psychological ploy to undermine Spurs' confidence.

Whelan and Rush then inflicted a Wembley nightmare on poor Ray Clemence, who had to pick the ball out of his net twice in extra-time.

A grand departure

The 1982–83 season was to see Liverpool clinch their 14th League title and make it a hat-trick of Milk Cup triumphs.

But before the action began, Bob Paisley shook Anfield by announcing that after 43 years of service to Liverpool, he had decided to retire.

The club won the Championship at a canter, 11 points clear of Watford, and they made it to Wembley again for the Milk Cup Final.

Manchester United offered stiff opposition in the Final with an opening goal from Norman Whiteside. Alan Kennedy, hero of the European Cup triumph in Paris, thrashed an equaliser, and Ronnie Whelan gave Liverpool a 2–1 winning advantage in extra-time.

Bob Paisley was given the ultimate honour, by his team captain Graeme Souness, of receiving the Cup in the Royal Box, the first manager to mount Wembley's 39 steps.

Thirteen trophies in a nine year occupation of the Liverpool hot-seat made Bob Paisley the most successful manager in English and European football history.

Chapter Six

Kenny's Kings

JOE FAGAN's two seasons in charge of Liverpool as successor to Bob Paisley were to start in spectacular success and end in grim tragedy.

If Paisley was nervous of the job of stepping into Shankly's shoes a decade earlier, Fagan, aged 62, moved even more cautiously into the hot-seat after a quarter of a century of toil in the coaching shadows at Anfield.

Born in Liverpool, Fagan's playing career had been fought away from Merseyside. He had played for Manchester City and Bradford Park Avenue and had seen non-League service elsewhere in the North.

He had served as a coach at Rochdale before moving to Anfield as part of Shankly's 'boot room' staff. But this was the big one, the toughest assignment of his career – and the critics were even more sceptical about his chances than they had been about Paisley's hopes of emulating Shankly.

The ink had hardly dried on his contract before Fagan had plunged into the transfer market for £300,000 to buy Gary Gillespie, Coventry's Scotland Under-21 defender.

Michael Robinson, highly prized by Brighton,

was signed for £200,000 and Europe's strongest club squad set out to try for a hat-trick of League titles, a feat not performed since the Second World War and only by Arsenal and Huddersfield before it.

By November Liverpool had hit the top spot and by April they were Champions again, with Ian Rush carving defences to ribbons in hammering 32 League goals and a total haul for the season of 45.

In spite of being knocked out of the F.A. Cup in the second round, the team strode confidently to their fourth Milk Cup Final against Everton. The big day at Wembley, dampened by pouring rain and poor football, ended all square and the two Mersey giants fought out a replay at Maine Road, Manchester.

This time Liverpool surged to a record fourth Milk Cup win by courtesy of Graeme Souness's powerful shot in the 22nd minute.

High hopes

Joe Fagan now reflected on the possibility that he could become the first manager to steer a Football League team to victory in three major Cup tournaments.

AS Roma stood between Liverpool and that remarkable achievement when the Reds swept into the Olympic stadium in Rome for the 1984 European Cup Final.

Fagan's squad were clearly confident of succeeding on their return to the scene of their victory over Borussia, but Roma had a distinct advantage in parading their talents on their home pitch.

Phil Neal, that veteran of so many European campaigns, shot the Reds into a 15th minute lead as Liverpool's 20,000 travelling supporters struggled to be heard above exploding fire-crackers and smoke-bombs.

Pruzzo equalised just before half-time and Grobbelaar needed all his sharpness to keep Liverpool's hopes alive in the second half. Sadly, the game moved into a penalty shoot-out after 120 minutes of deadlock.

Only the strongest competitors could survive. Liverpool looked to be dead if not buried when Steve Nicol drove his spot kick over Tancredi's crossbar, but Neal was more successful, and the spoils were equal when on Roma's second shot, Bruno Conti fluffed his kick.

Souness, Righetti and Rush all hit the net to make it 3–2 to Liverpool, but what was this? Bruce Grobbelaar, the most colourful recruit for years, was playing the clown as Graziani prepared to shoot. The Italian missed – and Alan Kennedy, a great Euro match-winner, won the game with a sizzling drive.

Grobbelaar revealed the secret of his psychological warfare game with Graziani. 'I put on my Ali-shuffle act, wobbling my knees and letting my head and arms loll as if I were desperately tired and about to drop to the ground.'

Joe Fagan was one of the last to leave the Olympic stadium that night. He lingered on to soak up the atmosphere.

That night Liverpool's heroes drank champagne long into the Italian night in their hotel above Rome. Several hundred Koppites joined them, but down in the streets of the famous city other Liverpool fans were being attacked by marauding groups of Roma fans.

The captain departs

Liverpool started their 1984–85 campaign without the services of their captain Graeme Souness. He left Anfield for Sampdoria in a £500,000 deal. He took with him memories of 250 League games, a string of medals, and his firm establishment as Scotland captain after more than 40 appearances.

Ready to fight for the vacancy in Liverpool's midfield were new recruits John Wark, from Ipswich, Jan Molby, a Dutch international from Ajax, and Kevin MacDonald, Leicester City's midfield star.

The Reds failed to win a trophy for the first time in nine years. They never looked capable of catching Everton in the League but surged to the F.A. Cup semi-finals where they went down to Manchester United in a replay.

Spurs bombed them out of the Milk Cup, so they turned to Europe again for success in the European Cup. Lech Poznan, Benfica, crushed by an Ian Rush hat-trick, then FK Austria Memphis and Panathinaikos were routed in Liverpool's confident assault on the European Cup and a meeting in the Final with the mighty Italian giants Juventus.

The Heysel outrage

A sunny evening in the Heysel Stadium, Brussels, gave a misleading introduction to events that were to cause severe damage to the reputation of all English clubs.

A television audience of millions witnessed a horror show in their own living rooms as Liverpool and Juventus supporters clashed in a bloody riot that left 39 people dead and hundreds injured.

A wall collapsed as Liverpool supporters broke through a barrier to chase Juventus fans. Some died instantly beneath debris and a panic-stricken crowd.

The emergency services swept into action. Stretchers were used to carry the dead and injured out of the Heysel hell-hole. Liverpool fans continued to taunt Juventus fans. Juventus fans continued to taunt Liverpool fans in an x-certificate screening to a world-wide television audience.

Arrests were made; the Heysel Stadium was condemned as inadequate for a major European Final; English clubs were banned from European competition; and Liverpool's reputation for fair play in a glorious crusade across Europe from Shankly to Fagan was destroyed in a crazy half hour of violence.

Never has the result of a major football Final meant less to the participants. Michel Platini scored, Juventus won, Liverpool lost, and nobody cared.

29 May 1985 will be marked forever as one of the foulest chapters in football history.

Mark Lawrenson, led off with injury in the first minute of the game, observed: 'What all the Liverpool players on duty that day have in common is the feeling of shock, and although it took time for the full significance to sink in we will carry that experience with us for the rest of our lives.'

Bruce Grobbelaar recalls a little girl limping out of the stadium 'searching for who knows what. Her lost shoe? A father? A brother? I wish I knew.'

The great Liverpool goalkeeper later revealed that he came within an inch of quitting the game after the Brussels disaster.

One man did quit – in tears. The Brussels disaster was too much for Joe Fagan. He had spoken unofficially of the European Cup Final being his last game in charge; but the events at the Heysel were to send him into retirement at the age of 64, disillusioned with football and its violent following.

A fresh start

Lesser clubs than mighty Liverpool would have allowed the tragic events of Brussels and the departure of their manager to upset their winning rythmn.

The Reds started the 1985–86 season with a new boss, Kenny Dalglish, and optimistic hopes of recovering from the biggest nightmare in their history.

Dalglish's appointment had surprised many experts, but with Bob Paisley promising to support the new young general from behind the scenes, the Anfield hierarchy were confident of a smooth transition.

Dalglish, the first player to score 100 goals in both the Scottish and English Leagues, and soon to be the first player to win 100 Scotland caps, led

Joe Fagan who retired after the Heysel Stadium disaster.

his team onto the Anfield pitch at the start of the 1985–86 season.

Long-serving defenders Phil Neal and Alan Kennedy were on the way out but Steve McMahon, once on Everton's books, was signed from Aston Villa to add strength to an already formidable midfield.

Liverpool were forced to trail in the First Division wake of Manchester United, who had bolted to the top of the table in a flurry of goals from their dynamic Welsh striker Mark Hughes. Then Everton took up the running, but the Reds tracked them all the way to a climactic finish to the Championship.

Liverpool simply had to beat Chelsea to win the title for a record 16th time. Who better to steer them to triumph than Kenny Dalglish? He created a television spectacular, catching a flighted cross on his chest and racing into Chelsea's penalty area before crashing the goal that won the title.

Liverpool and Everton were to be drawn together in the 1986 F.A. Cup Final, the first all-Mersey Final. For an hour it looked as if Everton would win their second Final in three successive Wembley appearances.

England striker Gary Lineker put Everton ahead, but Jan Molby, the Dutch master, set up Ian Rush for an equaliser.

Molby performed miracles again to make an opening for Craig Johnston, and with Everton pressing forward desperately for an equaliser, Whelan surged free on the left to offer Rush the perfect opening for his second goal.

Sadly for Everton, the law which dictated that

Liverpool never lost when Rush scored, had been proved true again.

Dalglish had led Liverpool to their first League and Cup Double in his first season.

Strains of 'You'll Never Walk Alone' rang round the Wembley terracing as the Kop again paid its moving tribute to the late Bill Shankly.

Rush's last stand

Liverpool and their great Merseyside rivals Everton were to fight out another fiercely contested First Division campaign in 1986–87. This time Everton were to clinch the title by nine clear points, with Ian Rush piling on the agony with 30 League goals. This was his last season at Anfield before moving to Juventus.

Rush smashed his 202nd goal for Liverpool in the Littlewoods Cup Final against Arsenal, but for the first time the Reds were to fail to win a game in which he had scored.

A two-goal burst by Charlie Nicholas destroyed Kenny Dalglish's side as they crashed to a 2–1 defeat.

Rush was to score his 207th and final goal for Liverpool in his final game – a 3–3 draw at Chelsea.

The League Centenary season

Liverpool's start to the 1987–88 campaign was staggering even by their impeccable standards.

John Aldridge, recruited from Oxford the previous season as replacement for Ian Rush, proved his worth by scoring in the first game of the season at Arsenal.

Steve Nicol, now emerging as a major force,

stole the show at Highbury in a 2–1 victory. He set the Reds on an astonishing unbeaten run of 29 League matches.

Mighty Liverpool, the great untouchables, made the Football League's centenary season memorable with their run of success in the League.

Barnes and Beardsley became the greatest threat to First Division defences for years, and even non-supporters became aware of the 'terrible twins'.

'Kenny's Kings' set the game alight with an explosive formula of power football. His team attacked every record in sight. Liverpool's brilliance inspired the legendary former England wing wizard Tom Finney to utter nine simple words that said it all: 'Liverpool must be the best team of all time.'

Even before the season started, the club tore the transfer record to shreds with the double signing of Peter Beardsley and John Barnes – £2.9 million worth of talent.

Liverpool soared to a record-breaking 17th League title, and on their way they equalled Leeds United's 1973–74 unbeaten start of 29 games.

They pulled in bigger gates and higher receipts than any other club in the 1987–88 season. They also smashed the club record of nine successive clean sheets.

Alan Hansen, the captain, confirmed his reputation as the Rolls-Royce of First Division defenders.

Steve McMahon, in midfield, burst into the England squad for the 1988 European Championships to join Liverpool team-mates Beardsley and Barnes.

Aldridge couldn't stop scoring, scoring one of the two winning goals to overpower Nottingham Forest and put them in the F.A. Cup Final, which was, sadly, lost to hard-working underdogs Wimbledon 1–0.

One of the few disappointments of an incredible season was Liverpool's defeat by Everton in their 30th League game, the one match that would have given them the ascendency over Leeds United, whose run of 29 League games had remained unbeaten since 1974.

Many thought the defeat would damage Dalglish's mighty charge towards the Championship. They couldn't have been more wrong.

Liverpool finally wrapped up the Championship, their 17th, by defeating Spurs at Anfield.

Record-signing Beardsley clinched the winning goal and delivered a warning: 'I have four more years here yet and I am looking for three or four more Championships.'

Who is to say that with a man of Kenny Dalglish's credentials at the helm, Liverpool are not capable of living up to Tom Finney's tag – TEAM OF THE CENTURY?

Chapter Seven

Ten of the Best

Billy Liddell
BILLY LIDDELL was the first of a long line of great wingers to thrill post-war crowds at Anfield. Liddell, Alan A'Court, Peter Thompson, Ian Callaghan, Steve Heighway and John Barnes have all given successive Liverpool attacks the width, pace and flair necessary to crack the most solid League defences.

Short, powerful, brave – if not lethal – Liddell was every schoolboy's hero in the North West just after the Second World War. He signed for Liverpool as an 18-year-old winger from Lochgelly Viollet, Dunfermline in July 1938. In less than two years he had convinced the Liverpool hierarchy that he was a match-winner.

He made his Liverpool début in a 7–1 rout of Crewe on New Year's Day 1940. A week later he smashed a hat-trick past the great Frank Swift in a 7–3 victory over Manchester City.

Liddell, never overawed by the big occasion, celebrated his League début in 1946–47 by scoring twice against Chelsea. One of the goals was a brilliant individual effort.

Liverpool's attacking trio of Liddell, Albert Stubbins and Jack Balmer were as merciless in the

Reds' Championship winning season of 1946–47 as Barnes, Beardsley and Aldridge were in Liverpool's title winning year of 1987–88. Liddell had gained eight Scottish caps by the end of the War and went on to make 28 more appearances for Scotland between 1947–56.

He represented Great Britain against the Rest of Europe in 1947 and was hailed the hero of Liverpool's F.A. Cup semi-final victory over Everton in 1950, a Wembley Final they were to lose to Arsenal 2–0.

Liddell, the perfect sportsman and a Justice of the Peace in retirement, made a record 492 appearances – Ian Callaghan later broke that record – and demonstrated a Dalglish-type strike rate by bagging 216 goals. He was murderous from the penalty spot. In 44 penalty attempts for Liverpool, he scored from 36 spot kicks.

The ambitious South American club Colombia, combing Britain for star players after the War, begged Liddell to join them for a £2000 signing-on fee.

Thankfully, one of Liverpool's greatest ever wingers declined the invitation. He was loyal to the Reds – and continued to play a major part in their incredible success story.

Roger Hunt
Roger Hunt's Liverpool record speaks volumes for the contribution he made at Anfield in a brilliant 10 year career, stretching from 1959 to the late sixties. He scored more goals than any other player in Liverpool's history, and his 41 strikes in the League campaign of 1961–62 remains a club record.

Roger Hunt (left), ace marksman for the Reds for 10 years.

Hunt, who joined Liverpool as a 19 year-old straight out of National Service, scored an incredible 245 goals in his 401 appearances in the number eight shirt he made his own.

Big, fair haired, and powerful with broad shoulders, Hunt was shrewdly placed by manager Bill Shankly alongside his famous partner Ian St John. They were the perfect combination in the Toshack-Keegan, Barnes-Beardsley mould. Hunt's outstanding marksmanship was soon acknowledged by the Football Association, and he won the first of 34 England caps against Austria in 1962.

His no-nonsense style was never popular with the purists in England crowds but Alf Ramsey's support of the big Liverpool striker never wavered. The England manager's loyalty was never emphasised better than in England's World Cup winning year of 1966. Hunt played in all six matches of the campaign, scoring three goals.

Then, he had a World Cup winner's medal to place alongside his Championship medal of 1964 and F.A. Cup Winner's medal of 1965. (That game had seen the old double-act of Hunt and St John score the Liverpool goals that sank Leeds United.)

Hunt left Liverpool for Bolton in 1969. The Kop showed its full appreciation of his outstanding contribution when 56,000 supporters turned up at Anfield for his testimonial.

One of the more obscure highlights of Hunt's career was that his goal in Liverpool's 3–2 victory over Arsenal in 1972 was the first goal ever recorded by BBC Television's 'Match of the Day'.

Ian St John

Ian St John became a legend on Merseyside. The story went that if Jesus Christ joined Liverpool, Shankly would move Saint John to inside right.

He was Shankly's first major signing. The legendary Anfield boss had taken months trying to persuade the Liverpool board that if the Reds were ever to be great again they needed to spend money on good players. Shanks' persuasive tongue changed attitudes, and he dashed to Motherwell to sign St John in 1961 for £37,000.

St John's début in a Liverpool Senior Cup game against Everton was sensational. He scored a hat-trick. By the end of the season St John's flair had steered Liverpool out of the Second Division.

St John scored 19 goals in 1962–63 to prove that First Division football was as much to his liking as the Second.

He had won his first Scotland cap against Czechoslovakia in 1961 and went on to gain 13 more in the next four years. Many observers at the time considered St John's unique talents poorly rewarded by the Scotland selectors.

His finest hour in a brilliant Liverpool career was his match-winning goal against Leeds in the 1965 F.A. Cup Final.

The Final had drifted into extra-time when Hunt pounced to put Liverpool ahead. Billy Bremner equalised, but in the final stages of the extra period St John launched himself at an Ian Callaghan cross to dispatch a powerful header into the Leeds net.

Bill Shankly described St John as one of his finest signings. His qualities are best measured by the fact that Ian St John is still a Liverpool legend.

Ray Clemence

The consistency of Ray Clemence in Liverpool's goal from the late 1960s through the glorious seventies was a major factor in them rising from domestic Football League excellence to become one of Europe's great footballing teams.

His courage in plunging at the feet of onrushing forwards made Liverpool supporters wince at the prospect of their 'Clem' receiving a bad injury. His spectacular handling, rising high above the Liverpool defence to grab balls from the air, made him one of the First Division's safest goalkeepers and a certainty for England selection.

Born in Skegness, Lincolnshire on 5 August 1948, he played 470 League games for Liverpool after following in Kevin Keegan's footsteps from Scunthorpe in 1967.

His medal-haul over the next 15 years was to make a mockery of the paltry £20,000 that Shankly paid to recruit him. He won five Championship medals, three European Cup winners' medals, and an F.A. Cup and a League Cup winners' medal before joining Spurs in 1982.

His contest with the great Peter Shilton for the right to wear the England jersey did not prevent him from enjoying an outstanding international career. Former England striker Jimmy Greaves remarked: 'England have been lucky to have had two such great goalkeepers with their careers coinciding'.

Clemence made 61 England appearances between 1973 and 1984, five of those as a Spurs player. But he will be remembered on Merseyside as arguably the finest goalkeeper to pull on the Liverpool jersey.

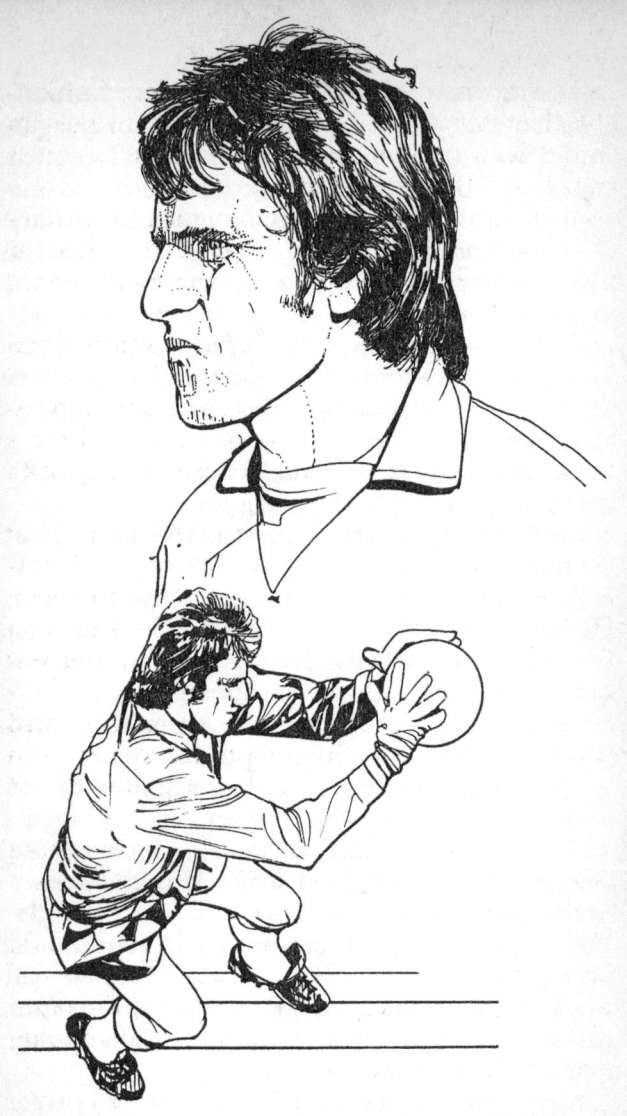

Ray Clemence, a consistently safe goalkeeper.

Kevin Keegan
In an era when work-rate became more fashionable than flair and individual skills, Kevin Keegan shone like a beacon across the Football League's rather drab features of the seventies.

Born in Armthorpe, Yorkshire on 14 February 1951, Keegan scored 68 goals in 230 games for Liverpool over a six year period from his début in 1971.

Heroes were fast going out of fashion when Liverpool plucked that little-known striker from the obscurity of Scunthorpe. Rejected by Coventry as too small, Keegan joined Liverpool for a mere £30,000 and went on to become England's best player over the next decade.

His brilliant individual performance against Borussia Moenchengladbach in the 1977 European Cup Final was his finest hour for Liverpool. He had previously scored two goals in the 1974 F.A. Cup Final victory over Newcastle, and was voted Footballer of the Year in 1976.

He moved to Hamburg for a British record transfer fee of £500,000 in 1977, and in 1979 and 1980 was twice elected European Footballer of the year.

Keegan wore the England shirt on 63 occasions between 1973 and the 1982 World Cup Finals.

His partnership with John Toshack in the Liverpool attack was sensational. Big John would knock the ball into Kevin's path and the ball would be nestling in the net. It worked the other way, too, with Keegan working as the supplier and Toshack the destroyer.

Kevin Keegan became a world class player through sheer effort. No player did more than him to establish Liverpool as one of Europe's greatest teams in the seventies.

Graeme Souness

Liverpool's post-war teams have all contained hard men. Tommy Smith was said to have been quarried from stone. If that was the case, then Graeme Souness must have been chipped from a Scottish peak near his Edinburgh birthplace!

If manager Bob Paisley needed a demolition job on a top European star, Souness was often the man to be chosen for the special assignment. He was one of Paisley's shrewdest signings, joining Liverpool from Middlesbrough for £350,000 in January 1978.

Given his chance to make the grade at Tottenham Hotspur, Souness had run away from White Hart Lane because of homesickness. He established himself as the general of Middlesbrough's midfield in 176 League appearances, and was hotly tipped to become a world class player if he could find the right club. Liverpool gave him that opportunity, and Souness returned the compliment by becoming the springboard for so many Reds' attacks in their glorious Championship, Cup and European campaigns of the late seventies and 1980s.

Souness won a host of medals for Liverpool, making his mark spectacularly in the 1978 European Cup Final victory over Bruges at Wembley by slotting the perfect pass for Kenny Dalglish to score his winning goal. He was a member of Liverpool's European Cup winning team of 1981, and picked up another European Cup winning medal against AS Roma in 1984. He won such acclaim as one of Europe's best midfield players that it came as no surprise when he moved to Italy and bade farewell to the Reds before the start of the 1984–85 season, after captaining them to three trophies.

The one-time wayward Scot had been transformed into a responsible, creative midfield powerhouse. The Genoa club Sampdoria were soon to warm to his talents before he turned to management, and Glasgow Rangers.

His former Liverpool team-mate Mark Lawrenson paid him this compliment: 'To outsiders he will always be remembered as one of the game's hard nuts . . . To sell him short by ignoring his skills in favour of the muscle would be the height of ignorance.'

Kenny Dalglish
The big talking point on Merseyside when Kevin Keegan left Liverpool for Hamburg in 1977 was: 'Who on earth can fill his boots?' It needed the greatest transfer coup in Liverpool's history to provide the answer.

Kenny Dalglish, the Crown Prince of Scottish League football, agreed to transfer his talents from Celtic to Anfield for a then record fee of £440,000.

He was 26, at the height of his powers, and had already made 40 appearances for his beloved Scotland. His goal-scoring record for Celtic was phenomenal – 112 goals in 204 League games. He grabbed a goal within seven minutes of his League début against Middlesbrough, and by the start of the 1987–88 season had cracked 118 League goals for the Reds in 352 appearances.

Kenny Dalglish, Liverpool player and now manager.

John Smith, the well respected Chairman of Liverpool, says: 'Kenny, as I have publicly stated previously, is our finest-ever signing as a player.'

He made the first of his record 102 Scotland appearances against Belgium as sub in 1972. He won his last cap against Luxembourg in 1987, bringing the curtain down on an incredible international career.

One of the greats of all time, he has featured in every one of Liverpool's record-breaking exploits in domestic and European competitions. He received the ultimate reward for his loyalty and outstanding services when he was asked to replace Joe Fagan as manager in May 1985.

Twice chosen as Footballer of the Year, Dalglish, who was awarded the MBE for his services to football, is clearly destined to become one of the great managers. At the end of his first season in charge, Liverpool had done the League and Cup Double.

Ian Rush

Ian Rush joined Liverpool as an 18-year-old striker in the 1979–80 season. He left the club in June 1986 in a record £3,200,000 transfer deal.

Born in St Asaph, Wales, Rush's goal-scoring talents began to blossom in 34 League appearances for Chester in which he scored 14 goals.

Bob Paisley took his time to draft the young Rush into Liverpool's first team, but once there, he cracked 139 goals in 224 League appearances for the Reds.

He won every honour in the game over a six year reign as the King of the Kop.

Tall and lean, his greyhound pace and unerring eye for the target made him the First Division's most explosive goal poacher in the Jimmy Greaves class. He could seize an opening in a flash, with that unique ability to bring the ball under control with just one touch.

If Ian Rush scored, Liverpool would go unbeaten. It was 'Rushie' who routed Everton in the 1986 F.A. Cup Final, enabling Liverpool to clinch the magic League and Cup Double. He scored two goals that day.

He was voted Liverpool's 'Young Player of the Year' in 1982–83 and became 'Player of the Year' in 1984.

Rush's Liverpool team-mate Bruce Grobbelaar says this of his chum: 'There is never going to be another like him. The nearest I have seen is Gary Lineker. Both have blinding speed and are natural goalscorers with Rush just earning my vote . . .'

Rush played for Wales from the moment he made his first Liverpool appearance, and by the end of his Liverpool career had won more than 30 caps.

Ian Rush found life difficult on arrival in Italy. He lost form in his first season with Juventus; but such is the Welshman's prodigious appetite for goals that his barren spell with be a minor interruption in the goal-busting exploits.

John Barnes

John Barnes was discovered by a Watford scout, playing football in a park.

Born in Jamaica in November 1963, Barnes began his senior football career playing before a handful of spectators for Sudbury Court. But the Watford manager Graham Taylor had always had an eye for talent, and no player rewarded his scouting system more than the brilliant Barnes. He made his Watford début in 1981 and went on to become a supercharged striker in the little club's march to League and Cup triumph.

His wing wizardry soon alerted England manager Bobby Robson, and in 1983 he made his full international début against Northern Ireland. By

1987 Barnes had made more than 30 appearances for England, often fighting Chris Waddle to be the winger in Robson's line-up.

Liverpool tracked Barnes for several seasons before Kenny Dalglish plunged boldly into the transfer market in a £900,000 deal in the summer of 1987.

If Barnes was exceptional in Watford's colours, he was soon to become sensational at Anfield.

For week after week in Liverpool's record-equalling unbeaten run of 29 League games in 1987–88, Barnes was man of the match.

His blistering runs down the left touchline were to send the Kop into raptures. His wing bursts would end with a measured cross to John Aldridge or Peter Beardsley, or, more often than not, Barnes would cut into the penalty box for a crack at goal himself.

Not since the days of Heighway and Thompson had Anfield seen such devilry from a Liverpool winger.

He ended 1987–88 as Liverpool's Man of the Season – possibly *any* season!

His price in the transfer market had rocketed to well over £1 million, but Liverpool were not selling their most precious asset.

Peter Beardsley
Peter Beardsley's rags-to-riches story is a lesson for any youngster aspiring to make the grade.

The Geordie-born Beardsley joined Carlisle United at 18. For three summers he travelled to Canada to play for Vancouver Whitecaps, returning in the winter to play for Carlisle, then Manchester United, and finally Newcastle United.

Only at Newcastle did the full range of his talents begin to blossom. He signed for the 'Magpies' in 1983, responded enthusiastically to the promptings of former Liverpool star Kevin Keegan, and did as much as anyone to see Newcastle to promotion from the Second Division. His willingness to play the sharp early ball, his first great touch, mazy dribbling skills, pace and accuracy carried him into so many goal-scoring positions that he could hardly fail.

Twenty-two goals in 122 League appearances for Newcastle persuaded Kenny Dalglish to part with £2 million for Beardsley in summer 1987. His arrival at Anfield and partnership with his England colleague John Barnes brought breathtaking rewards in their first season with Liverpool in 1987–88.

Nicknamed 'Ceefax' because of his incredible knowledge of football history, Beardsley's all-action enthusiasm in the England shirt prompted coach Don Howe to comment: 'He might as well be captain – he does everything else on the pitch.'

That sums up Beardsley's contribution as one of football's most popular players. Some of his goals in his first Liverpool season were superb, carved from nothing, and rocketed into opponents' nets with the minimum of backlift.

He won his place in the England squad just before the 1986 World Cup, and forged an outstanding partnership with Gary Lineker.

Kenny Dalglish's money was well-spent, but if Beardsley maintains his phenomenal rate of progress as Britain's most expensive player, who knows what transfer fee he could command in the years ahead?

Index

Ajax 41
Aldridge, John 77, 79
Allan, George 12
Anfield 12
Aston Villa 13

Balmer, Jack 22
Barnes, John 7, 78, 92–3
Beardsley, Peter 7, 78, 93–4
Becton, Frank 12
Borussia Dortmund 40
Borussia Moenchengladbach 48, 58–60
Bradshaw, Harry 12
Busby, Matt 18
Byrne, Gerry 30, 34

Callaghan, Ian 30, 34, 81
Celtic 39–40
Chelsea 33–4
Clemence, Ray 42, 43, 66, 85–6
Cologne 37
Cup Final, 1914 15–16
 1965 34
 1971 45
 1974 49
 1977 57–8
 1986 76–7

Dalglish, Kenny 8, 60, 61, 62, 74–7, 79, 89–91
Doig, Ned 14

English, Sammy 19
European Cup 36–9, 49, 52, 57, 58–60, 61–2, 64–6, 70, 72–4
European Cup-Winners' Cup 39–40, 41, 52
Evans, Alun 44
Everton 11, 17, 19, 41

FA Cup 14, 15, 34, 35, 39, 49, 76
Fagan, Joe 8, 69–74
Fagan, Willie 23
Fairclough, David 54–5, 57
Fairs Cup 42, 43, 44, 48
Football League 10, 11, 16

Greaves, Jimmy 47
Grobbelaar, Bruce 7, 66, 71, 74

Hansen, Alan 7, 60, 78
Hardy, Sam 14
Harrop, James 15
Hateley, Tony 42
Heighway, Steve 43
Hewitt, Joe 14
Heysel Stadium 8, 72–4

95

Hodgson, Gordon 18
Houlding, John 13
Howell, Rab 12
Hughes, Emlyn 41–2, 60, 62
Hughes, Laurie 24
Hunt, Roger 30, 34, 35, 40, 81–3

Inter Milan 37–9

Jackson, Rev. James 18
Johnson, David 55–6
Juventus 72–3

Kay, George 20, 22, 24
Keegan, Kevin 29, 45–7, 54, 55, 56, 60, 87–8
Kennedy, Alan 64
Kennedy, Ray 50, 54
Kop 9

Lancashire Association 10
Lawler, Chris 39
Lawrence, Tommy 32
Lawrenson, Mark 73–4
League Championship 7, 13, 14, 17, 33, 48, 52, 54, 57, 63, 67, 68, 76, 79
League Cup 61
Liddell, Billy 7, 19, 20–26, 80–81
Longworth, Ephraim 15
Louis, Joe 20

Manchester United 16
McDermott, Terry 54
McKenna, John 10, 12, 13, 17
McQueen, Matt 17
McVean, Malcolm 10, 11
Melia, Jimmy 25

Milk Cup 63–4, 67–8, 70
Milne, Gordon 30
Molby, Jan 76
Moran, Ronnie 26

Neal, Phil 54, 71
Newcastle United 49
Nicol, Steve 71, 77–8

Paisley, Bob 22, 24, 51–60, 63, 68

Raisbeck, Alex 7, 12–13, 14, 15
Rush, Ian 7, 63, 67, 70, 77, 91–2

Scott, Elisha 7, 15, 17
Shankly, Bill 8, 26, 27–35, 50, 51, 66
Souness, Graeme 61, 62, 64, 72, 88–9
Spion Kop 9, 14
St Etienne 57
St John, Ian 31, 34, 84
Stubbins, Albert 7, 22

Taylor, Phil 24, 25
Thomson, John 19
Thompson, Peter 32–3, 34
Thompson, Phil 49–50
Toshack, John 43, 54, 55, 56, 62
Twentyman, Geoff 25

UEFA Cup 48–9, 52, 55

Watson, Tom 9, 13
Welsh, Don 24
World Cup 35

Yeats, Ron 31, 32, 34